Pinterest™ Marketing
FOR
DUMMIES®

by Kelby Carr

WILEY

John Wiley & Sons, Inc.

Pinterest™ Marketing For Dummies®

Published by
John Wiley & Sons, Inc.
111 River Street
Hoboken, NJ 07030-5774

www.wiley.com

WILEY

About the Author

Kelby Carr is the founder and CEO of Type-A Parent (www. typeaparent.com), a social network and online magazine-style blog founded in 2007 for parent bloggers, and Type-A Parent Conference (www.typeaconference.com), an annual blogging and social media conference founded in 2009 that attracts major corporations and hundreds of parents who blog. She is a social media and blogger outreach consultant. She is a frequent speaker on new media topics.

She's been coding since 1982, social networking online since 1984, web publishing since 1992, blogging since 2002, and tweeting since 2007. She was an early adopter of Pinterest, and is active there daily with thousands of followers and hundreds of pins.

You can follow her on Twitter at @typeamom (http://twitter. com/typeamom), find her on Facebook at http://facebook. com/kelby, and, of course, follow her personal Pinterest account at http://pinterest.com/kelby and her business account at http://pinterest.com/typeacon.

Dedication

This book is dedicated to my husband and three children. They are my world, and I would even give up the Internet for them. Fortunately, they haven't asked me to. Yet.

Author's Acknowledgments

Thank you to Ellen Gerstein for being a great friend and for making this happen, to Amy Fandrei for sealing the deal, to Linda Morris for the great editing, and to Melanie Nelson for having one of the hottest brains I know (and for killer technical editing). I also want to acknowledge the many smart and talented business people, entrepreneurs, public relations people, and marketing gurus I call friends who are a constant source of knowledge and information about this fascinating world of social media.

Publisher's Acknowledgments

We're proud of this book; please send us your comments at http://dummies.custhelp.com. For other comments, please contact our Customer Care Department within the U.S. at 877-762-2974, outside the U.S. at 317-572-3993, or fax 317-572-4002.

Some of the people who helped bring this book to market include the following:

Acquisitions and Editorial

Project Editor: Linda Morris

Acquisitions Editor: Amy Fandrei

Copy Editor: Linda Morris

Technical Editor: Melanie Nelson

Editorial Manager: Jodi Jensen

Editorial Assistant: Leslie Saxman

Sr. Editorial Assistant: Cherie Case

Cover Photo: © kizikayaphotos/iStockphoto.com

Cartoons: Rich Tennant (www.the5thwave.com)

Composition Services

Project Coordinator: Patrick Redmond

Layout and Graphics: Jennifer Creasey, Lavonne Roberts

Proofreader: Rebecca Denoncour

Indexer: Palmer Publishing Services

Publishing and Editorial for Technology Dummies

    Richard Swadley, Vice President and Executive Group Publisher

    Andy Cummings, Vice President and Publisher

    Mary Bednarek, Executive Acquisitions Director

    Mary C. Corder, Editorial Director

Publishing for Consumer Dummies

    Kathleen Nebenhaus, Vice President and Executive Publisher

Composition Services

    Debbie Stailey, Director of Composition Services

Contents at a Glance

Introduction *1*

Chapter 1: Understanding Why You Need a Pinterest Presence................... 5

Chapter 2: Setting Up a Pinterest Account 17

Chapter 3: Following People on Pinterest 37

Chapter 4: Creating Boards and Pins 59

Chapter 5: Pinning and Repinning 79

Chapter 6: Getting Active on Pinterest 95

Chapter 7: Getting Fans, Customers, and Clients to Follow You 105

Chapter 8: Engaging on Pinterest 123

Chapter 9: Creating Pin-Worthy Content 133

Chapter 10: Generating Buzz on Pinterest... 153

Chapter 11: Tracking Pinterest Metrics 163

Chapter 12: Ten Pins That Went Viral... 173

Index *183*

Table of Contents

Introduction 1
About This Book 1
How This Book Is Organized 2
Foolish Assumptions... 3
Icons Used in This Book 3
Where to Go from Here... 4

Chapter 1: Understanding Why You Need a Pinterest Presence 5
Knowing the Business Benefits of Pinterest.................................5
Understanding Pinterest Demographics 8
Setting Goals and a Mission for Your Pinterest Profile...............9
Determining How to Best Represent Your Brand on Pinterest 10
Understanding Copyright and Legal Issues 14

Chapter 2: Setting Up a Pinterest Account 17
Deciding Whether to Use a Business or Personal Identity....................17
Deciding Who Should Run Your Pinterest Account...................20
Getting an Invitation to Join Pinterest 22
Maintaining Control of Your Pinterest Account 25
Setting Up Your New Account..26
    Setting up your profile...28
    Adding a profile picture 31
    Adding a bio...32
    Setting your e-mail preferences 33
Understanding the Social Etiquette for Businesses on Pinterest...........34
Understanding the Pinterest Lingo 35

Chapter 3: Following People on Pinterest 37
Using Pinterest Site and Search to Find People to Follow.......................38
    Using Pinterest search to find people to follow...............................38
    Using Pinterest categories and Popular pins to find
        people to follow...42
    Using Pinterest Everything stream to find people to follow 45
    Using Pinterest Friend and Follower lists to find people 47
    Following your followers back 48
Finding Facebook Friends to Follow 50
Finding E-mail Contacts to Follow 55
More Tips on Finding People to Follow 57

Chapter 4: Creating Boards and Pins **59**

Creating Boards 59
Naming your board 62
Choosing a category 63
Creating a new board 63
Creating collaborative group boards 64
Rearranging Your Boards 71
Editing Your Board Cover Photo 72
Editing Your Boards 75
Deleting a Board 76
Leaving a Collaborative Board 76

Chapter 5: Pinning and Repinning **79**

Adding a Pin with a Website URL 79
Installing the Pinterest Pin It Button 82
Using the Pin It Button to Add a Pin 83
Uploading an Image as a Pin 84
Repinning 86
Finding pins to repin 87
Sharing a pin or repin on Facebook and Twitter 88
Using Hashtags, Mentions, and Price Tags 90
Using hashtags 90
Tagging member names in pins 91
Including a price tag in a pin 92

Chapter 6: Getting Active on Pinterest **95**

Finding Time for Pinterest 95
Setting a Pinterest Schedule 96
Finding Shareable Content to Pin 97
Commenting and Liking 100

Chapter 7: Getting Fans, Customers, and Clients to Follow You **105**

Using Your Website, E-mail List, and Social Media Channels
to Attract Followers 106
Promoting your Pinterest profile on your website or blog 106
Promoting your Pinterest profile in your e-mail marketing 112
Using social networks to attract Pinterest followers 115
Integrating Pinterest into Print and Broadcast Marketing Efforts 117
Attracting Pinterest Followers at Your Store or Location 118
Participating in Pinterest-Related Content and Link Lists
on Other Sites 122

Chapter 8: Engaging on Pinterest 123
Understanding What Is Engaging on Pinterest 123
Creating a Pin That Will Get Repinned 126
Creating a Pin That Encourages Comments 128
Handling Trolls, Spammers, and Negative or Inappropriate
Interaction 130
Being a Good Pinterest Citizen 132

Chapter 9: Creating Pin-Worthy Content 133
Finding Your Content That Has Been Shared on Pinterest 133
Making It Easy to Pin Your Images 135
Adding the Pin It web button 135
Adding a WordPress Pin It plug-in 137
Installing the Pinterest "Pin It" Button plug-in 141
Creating Pin-Friendly Images 143
Handling Image Pinning Issues 146
Watermarking your images 146
Reporting a copyright violation 149
Blocking pinning of your images 151

Chapter 10: Generating Buzz on Pinterest 153
Engaging with Your Brand Enthusiasts 153
Running Successful Pinterest Marketing Campaigns 155
Deciding Whether to Use Pin It to Win It Campaigns 158

Chapter 11: Tracking Pinterest Metrics .163
Using Analytics and Statistics Programs to Track Traffic Referrals 163
Tracking Followers, Repins, and Likes 167
Creating a Pinterest Measurement Report 168

Chapter 12: Ten Pins That Went Viral 173
Chocolate Chip Cookie Recipe Pin 173
Harry Potter Light Switch Pin 174
Bed and Breakfast Bathroom Pin 174
Pretty Updo Pin 176
He's Quite Perfect Pin 176
Balsamic Watermelon Cubes Pin 177
How to Frost a Cupcake Pin 179
How to Make a Clementine Candle Pin 179
Water Candle Pin 180
Camibands Pin 181

Index *183*

Introduction

• •

*P*interest is an overnight online marketing sensation. The social bookmarking site has quickly risen from obscurity to become the third most popular social network. The site, which is an image-driven virtual pinboard, is now attracting visits and members in the millions. Beyond that, it is driving traffic to websites in droves.

The site's meteoric rise has captured the attention of many businesses, agencies, and brands as they discover the intense impact of going viral on Pinterest. In fact, for some companies, simply a steady, consistent presence on Pinterest has translated into massive amounts of new visitors to their own sites.

Pinterest is still quite new. It launched in 2010 and remains in invitation-only beta status as of this writing. Regardless, the site became a top 10 social media site in December of 2011. By March of 2012, web metrics companies like Experian Hitwise (`www.experian.com/blogs/hitwise/`) and comScore (`www.comscore.com`) declared it to be the third most popular social network behind only Facebook and Twitter.

About This Book

This book serves as an instruction manual on joining Pinterest, as well as a course in etiquette for a business seeking to use Pinterest for marketing. It provides tips on building and nurturing a following and encouraging participation and engagement.

It discusses Pinterest campaigns and contests, as well as some important considerations before you launch into marketing campaigns headfirst without considering the implications (some members of Pinterest, for example, find the new rash of "pin it to win it" contests to be highly irritating).

You may even think you can look at how others are using Pinterest to get ideas for your own marketing. The majority of companies on Pinterest, however, are doing it poorly. This book gives you solid advice on how to not only exist on Pinterest but to co-exist, and to not just talk about yourself, but to listen.

I also use a few conventions you should be aware of. Text you should type is in **boldface**. New terms appear in *italic*. Web addresses look like this: `www.pinterest.com`. Placeholder text in a web address is in a special font and italic, like this: `www.`*`yourdomain`*`.com`. When you see a web address italicized in this way, you should replace the italic text with information pertinent to your website.

How This Book Is Organized

Chapters 1-4 teach the basic hows and whys of Pinterest for marketing. Find out why you need a Pinterest presence, why so many companies are jumping on Pinterest, and what the ROI (return on investment) is. You also learn how to discover your Pinterest personality to best showcase your business. These chapters also cover the important topics of copyright and other legal issues.

Learn some key considerations as you set up your account and all the basic instructions to get registered and get a profile up and running. Understand Pinterest etiquette and lingo, and find people to follow on Pinterest. In these chapters, you also create your first boards and pins. Boards are collections of pins under a subject or topic set by you, and pins are images you pin to a board.

There is so much more to Pinterest marketing than just joining and throwing up some boards. In Chapters 5-7, you'll learn about getting active on Pinterest, including finding time to use the social network during a busy day. Get tips on finding great images to pin and repin and interacting with likes and comments. You will also find tips on growing a following among your customers and clients using both online and offline tools.

In these chapters, learn not only how to use Pinterest but also how to encourage other members to engage with you: to repin, to like, and comment. Also get tips on reporting bad behavior and being a polite and well-liked member of the Pinterest community.

If you're reading this book, you want more than a presence on Pinterest. You want some spectacular results. Chapters 8-10 cover creating your own content that is pin-worthy as well as easy for others to share on Pinterest. Find out how to optimize images on your own site or blog to be pinnable and how to build Pinterest traffic with content on your own site. You will also learn some tricks to find out which of your content, products, and web pages other members have shared on Pinterest.

Discover how to go viral on Pinterest and the keys to successful marketing campaigns on Pinterest.

Chapter 11 delves into ways to measure the results of your Pinterest efforts, including tracking metrics and examining your site's analytics to determine traffic, sales, or other goals you set for your Pinterest marketing. You also learn how Pinterest impacts your own site's search engine optimization (SEO) and how to identify your best brand enthusiasts through your site's statistics.

In Chapter 12, discover ten pins that went viral.

Foolish Assumptions

If you're reading this book, I am assuming you have some basic understanding of social media. Although it isn't necessary, it is helpful if you are already using Facebook and Twitter to promote your business or organization. An understanding of basic marketing concepts isn't necessary either, but it certainly will be helpful.

You will, however, need to have a basic understanding of using the Internet. The instructions in this book are step by step for getting set up and using Pinterest, but I can't cover here basic instruction on how to use your computer, the Internet, or your mobile device (if you will use Pinterest on mobile).

For certain instructions in Chapters 9-10, I assume you either are highly comfortable poking around the backend of your site or blog or you have a webmaster you can send tasks to who is familiar with basic web development and HTML. For Chapter 11, I assume you have basic analytics set up for your site or blog and a basic familiarity with reading the results and statistics there.

What I do not assume is precisely why you want to read this book. You may be a small business or blog that simply wants to see a nice traffic boost from Pinterest (or even find some inspiration there or socialize). You could be the social media manager for a Fortune 500 company seeking to build a comprehensive Pinterest strategy for your company. In either situation, this book has all the core and crucial information you need to use Pinterest for marketing.

Icons Used in This Book

I use some basic icons throughout this book to help you quickly scan and find useful information and tips.

When you see the Tip icon, you know you're getting a quick tidbit of handy information on using Pinterest.

Some information is important to remember as you use Pinterest, so when you see this Remember icon, be sure to tuck the information away for future reference. Pinterest can be easy to use in mental autopilot mode, so this information is there to help as you navigate the site.

Watch out! As with any social network, you may need to avoid some pitfalls or do a vital task as you participate. Also, because Pinterest is new, I alert you to some need-to-know quirks.

If you love getting a peek at the geek, this icon is for you. Technical Stuff icons alert you when I'm sharing some technical details about Pinterest. If geek just isn't your thing, feel free to skip these — reading them isn't crucial to your understanding and use of Pinterest.

Where to Go from Here

The simplest route is to read this book in order, from beginning to end, but that certainly isn't mandatory. If you're brand new to Pinterest or will be setting up your account as you read this book, I recommend going in order. If you're already on Pinterest and simply want to understand the marketing potential there, feel free to jump around to the chapters and sections that interest you. After you read this book, keep it handy as you navigate Pinterest and use it as a reference as needed.

If you get stuck, have a question, or need any help, feel free to ask me! Like and interact with the Facebook *Pinterest Marketing For Dummies* page at www. facebook.com/PinterestMarketingForDummies, find me on Twitter at http://twitter.com/typeamom, and, of course, please follow me on Pinterest at http://pinterest.com/kelby for my personal profile and http://pinterest.com/typeacon for my business profile.

I also have a Pinterest board, Pinterest For Dummies, where I pin helpful articles and resources on Pinterest at http://pinterest.com/kelby/ pinterest-for-dummies, as well as a Pinterest Marketing For Dummies board, where I pin marketing tip articles and similar content, at http:// pinterest.com/kelby/pinterest-marketing-for-dummies.

Occasionally, we have updates to our technology books. If this book does have technical updates, they will be posted at dummies.com/go/pinterest marketingfdupdates.

Chapter 1

Understanding Why You Need a Pinterest Presence

In This Chapter

▶ Knowing the business benefits of Pinterest

▶ Setting goals for your Pinterest marketing

▶ Discovering your business's Pinterest personality

▶ Understanding copyright and other legal issues

Pinterest is a virtual pinboard. Although it is functionally a social book-marking site much like Digg (http://digg.com) and StumbleUpon (www.stumbleupon.com), the experience is much more aesthetic and visual than other sites of this genre. It is, in essence, a virtual version of a pinboard you might hang over your desk.

In this chapter, I cover the benefits that Pinterest can offer your business and urge you to set goals for your Pinterest marketing efforts. I also talk about how you can discover your business's "personality" on Pinterest, and give you some important copyright caveats.

Knowing the Business Benefits of Pinterest

When you share an image on Pinterest, each bookmark is called a *pin*. When you share someone else's pin on Pinterest, it's called a *repin*. You group pins together by topic onto various *boards* or *pinboards* in your profile. Each board mimics a real-life pinboard (see Figure 1-1). You can pin images by directly uploading them, or by pinning images you find online.

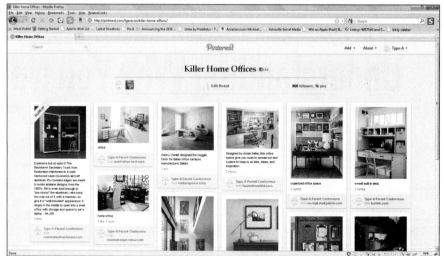

Figure 1-1:
A sample
pinboard, or
board, on
Pinterest.

Pinterest is still new enough that it isn't mainstream (yet), so your business doesn't *have* to be on Pinterest like customers might expect to find you on Twitter or Facebook. With Pinterest so quickly catching up with those top two social networking sites, however, those days may be here sooner than you think.

Beyond that, Pinterest is proving wildly effective at building interest and driving referring traffic to business and brand sites. In fact, Pinterest is driving more traffic referrals than Twitter, Google+, LinkedIn, and YouTube, according to statistics in February 2012 from Shareaholic (www.shareaholic.com), an online link sharing tool that handles millions of social referrals monthly.

Here are some of the benefits for businesses using Pinterest:

- ✔ **Shares of your own content and images can drive traffic to your site.** When an image is pinned from a website or blog, the image automatically links to the original site where it was pinned.

- ✔ **Being active on Pinterest provides businesses a chance to tell their story visually, which can be a very engaging method.**

- ✔ **Pinterest is a wonderful platform to showcase your brand's soul and personality.** Yes, you can share your products and content, but Pinterest also provides a great chance to show off other interests, to show your fans and potential customers what interests you share, and to allow your brand's personal side to shine.

✔ **It provides search engine optimization (SEO) benefits**. Although Pinterest has recently reduced some of the benefits by including no-follow coding on many links in pins, which means Google ignores the link, boards and pins do perform well in search results.

✔ **Pinterest is a site for discovery, which means you can be discovered.** Although people often use sites like search engines to look for something very specific, the fun of Pinterest is in finding what you never even knew you were looking for. That may sound nonsensical, but it means that your business, service, or product can be discovered, even by those who weren't planning to look for or buy it before they visited Pinterest. There is much to be said for capturing people's attention as it wanders.

✔ **It encourages businesses to create good, pin-worthy content.** One of the most overlooked benefits of Pinterest is that it is driving sites to create better content — not just better images but also better articles, tutorials, and blog posts.

Amazingly, Pinterest went from a largely unknown site rarely used by business to a booming success in just six months' time. Pinterest is the subject of dozens of news articles and blog posts daily.

To stay updated on the latest news and buzz on Pinterest, consider creating a Google Alert. To do so, visit `http://google.com/alerts` and use Pinterest as a keyword to track. You can set how often you receive Alerts, and whether you get Alerts from all sources or just certain types (see Figure 1-2).

Figure 1-2:
Setting up a
Google Alert
for the term
"Pinterest."

Understanding Pinterest Demographics

The typical Pinterest user is female. (Google Ad Planner's Pinterest profile claims 74 percent of users are female, although Experian data shows that just 60 percent of members are female.) Regardless of which statistic is correct, anyone active on Pinterest notices that women dominate.

The average income for users is in the $25,000-$49,999 range, and the most common age is between 35 and 44 years, according to Google Ad Planner data. One out of four Pinterest visitors has a college degree of some sort.

Geographically, Pinterest is used heavily in the middle of the U.S. In fact, according to Experian data, Pinterest recently beat out Facebook and Twitter in usage in Alabama, Oklahoma, Kansas, Utah, and Missouri.

The demographics describe a typical Pinterest user, but I want to remind you that Pinterest has a wide variety of members. It has a reputation as a site for crafty women from the Midwest, but that is just one segment. There are men on Pinterest (it's true, and they are a growing group), and there are popular pins related to a wide variety of topics, from social media statistics via info-graphics to *Star Wars* figurines.

It can be tempting to say that your business isn't about crafts or design, so why bother with Pinterest? My business has nothing to do with crafts or design, but I still find Pinterest to be highly valuable.

It is important to be aware of the demographic data on Pinterest, but don't let the data dictate your every move or scare you away from using Pinterest entirely. For example, the site is popular with women, yes. Deciding to appeal only to women, however, could be a mistake. Of the 100 million-plus visits to Pinterest in February, for example, about 25 million would have been men if the numbers reported are correct. That is a big chunk of people to ignore.

Demographics data can change frequently, especially with a site booming as rapidly as Pinterest is. You can find up-to-date numbers and estimates by keeping tabs on a few metrics-related blogs such as the Nielsen Wire at `http://blog.nielsen.com/nielsenwire` and Experian's Hitwise blog at `http://weblogs.hitwise.com`. You can also find demographic data by searching for Pinterest.com at `www.compete.com`, `www.quantcast.com`, `www.alexa.com` (see Figure 1-3) or `www.google.com/adplanner`. Be aware that in some cases, the data is an estimate and may not reflect reality.

Figure 1-3: Alexa's audience and demographics data estimates for Pinterest.

Setting Goals and a Mission for Your Pinterest Profile

Yes, Pinterest is there and it is all the rage right now, but those reasons alone are not adequate to justify joining. Instead, you should come up with at least a basic strategy. Even a simple note with a bulleted list of goals can be helpful in everything from determining your approach to measuring results later.

Some sample goals include

✔ **Boosting traffic.** You can set a specific goal of getting a certain number of monthly referrals from Pinterest, or set a goal to increase the percentage of referrals from Pinterest each month. In Chapter 11, I cover details about tracking these statistics.

✔ **Increasing sales.** You can use tools such as Google Analytics to track sales and revenue that directly are sourced from Pinterest referrals. In Chapter 11, I cover instructions on tracking conversions in Google Analytics.

✔ **Increasing brand awareness.** Your goal with Pinterest could be to make more people aware of your business in general, or to increase awareness of details about your business, your products or your services.

✔ **Identifying passionate brand evangelists**. It can be powerful to identify even a handful of brand enthusiasts, and Pinterest can be a great platform for doing so. I cover more details about how to identify and engage with your business' enthusiasts in Chapter 10.

✔ **Increasing engagement with customers and potential customers**. As a business, it can be easy to seem distant and lacking in connection for customers and clients. Pinterest, however, is a nice platform for showing off your brand's fun or quirky side, and to interact with your customers to get a sense for what they like.

✔ **Boosting buzz about your business.** You can use Pinterest to self-promote within reason. Beyond that, by making your own site, products and content easy to pin (and optimizing it so images will look good and be pinworthy), you will encourage others to spread the word. I cover tips on being easy to pin (and encouraging it) in Chapter 9.

Before you delve in, check out what some other brands are doing on Pinterest currently. Hundreds of businesses are already using Pinterest. On my site, you can find a list of more than 150 brands at `http://typeaparent.com/150-brands-on-pinterest.html`. Although many businesses don't use Pinterest effectively, browsing the brands currently on Pinterest for ideas of what to do and what not to do can be helpful.

Determining How to Best Represent Your Brand on Pinterest

Pinterest isn't just another place to shove products, services, and content down people's throats. It is the place to breathe life into your brand, to give it a distinct personality.

At first, it can seem uncomfortable to give your business a personality, so to speak. I felt awkward when I switched from using my personal account on Pinterest (where I just shared whatever I fancied) to my business account for Type-A Parent Conference.

As I got into the groove of sharing as a business rather than an individual, however, I found that I ended up having more fun with the business Pinterest account than the personal one. Yes, I am serious. Why? Because my business was truly developing its own passion, personality, and soul.

On Pinterest, it can be helpful to brainstorm random topics and ideas that you believe represent your business. These interest points for your brand can help you determine what boards to create, what content to pin and repin, and even what content to create on your own site or blog in the hopes of getting pinned and representing your business.

Here are a few questions to ask yourself as you feel around for your Pinterest business personality:

✔ **What topics are people such as my customers or readers passionate about?** Of those topics, which have a nice tie-in to my business? For this area, don't feel all topics must directly relate to your business. Sometimes, it is just a shared passion, such as science or reading. As an example, for my business site, I created a board of cool and creative business cards (see Figure 1-4). No, I don't sell business cards, but almost anyone attending my conference will buy them before they attend. This doesn't technically promote my business, but it is of high interest to my customers and, well, it is just a fun board that gets a lot of engagement.

✔ **What can you share about your business to humanize the business, that is unknown, unexpected, or behind the scenes?** With the ability to upload images directly to Pinterest, think of ways you can share what happens at your office, on the assembly line, with your employees, or in your travels. Is there a way to give people a view behind the curtain? The Weather Channel, for example, has a TWC Personalities board (`http://pinterest.com/weatherchannel/twc-personalities`) with fun images sent in from fans of meteorologists, as well as their own pictures of their personalities in the studio and out in the field (see Figure 1-5).

Figure 1-4: A business card board as a creative way to engage on my business Pinterest profile.

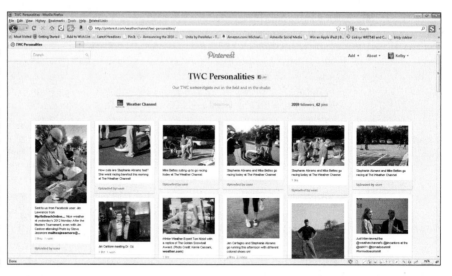

Figure 1-5: The Weather Channel shows off the lighter side of its meteorologists with its "TWC Personalities" board.

✔ **How can you share important information?** Although it is fun (and important) to be creative, you also want to remember to share important information and resources for your followers. It isn't as sexy as a wacky board, but be sure to have a board or boards for sharing latest news, basic instructions, tutorials and any other content, resources, or information that a customer, client, or reader would need.

✔ **How can you shine the spotlight on customers, partners, or readers?** A great way to engage and to draw attention to your business is to share cool images and content from your audience or customer base. Sony Electronics (http://pinterest.com/sonyelectronics), for example, has a board where they pin images shot with Sony cameras (see Figure 1-6).

✔ **How can you have fun?** Creativity is rewarded on Pinterest, so if you aren't having fun, you probably won't get as much engagement. Even if you have a pretty traditional business or a brand that has been around for decades (or centuries, even), you can find new and creative ways to share on Pinterest. Shoot, even stodgy ol' General Electric (http://pinterest.com/generalelectric) has a Badass Machines board. Little Debbie (http://pinterest.com/thelittledebbie), a classic American snack cake icon, has a board dedicated to Little Debbie Dessert Sushi (see Figure 1-7), which includes images as well as instructions on how to turn the low-priced snack cakes into upscale pretty desserts.

Figure 1-6:
Sony
Electronics
shares
photos shot
with their
cameras.

Figure 1-7:
Little
Debbie's
dessert
sushi board.

✔ **How can you share about your business in an interesting and unique way?** It is simple to just share images of the things you sell and hope people will buy. Honestly, anyone can do that. Besides the fact that oversharing self-promotional links is spammy (see more about this in Chapter 2), it isn't as effective at hooking your followers as a little dose of creativity is. Lilly Pulitzer (http://pinterest.com/lillypulitzer) features a board with images from various retail stores (see Figure 1-8), and Scholastic (http://pinterest.com/scholastic) has a board with old school books and pamphlets.

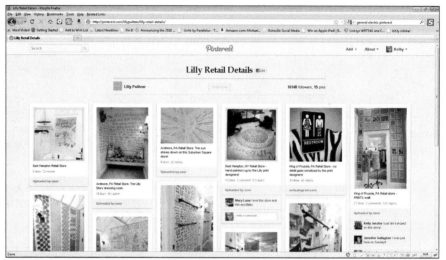

Figure 1-8:
Lilly
Pulitzer's
Lilly Retail
Details
board.

Understanding Copyright and Legal Issues

Before you even begin in Pinterest, you should be aware that the site has been troubled with copyright and other legal issues. Obviously, that hasn't stopped many companies from jumping rapidly on the Pinterest bandwagon. Still, as you progress, you may want to search Google for the latest news related to Pinterest and copyright. You also might consult a lawyer before you begin.

In Chapter 2, I share some etiquette tips. In many cases, following those tips not only allows you to be a polite community member but also helps you avoid legal pitfalls.

Pinterest in recent months has taken several steps to address some of the copyright concerns about the site. They have placed a 500-character limit on descriptions of images pinned, which now prevents members from reproducing entire posts with the image pinned. This tendency to post the entire text meant that no one needed to click through to the original source to get the copyrighted content. Pinterest has also completely revamped their Terms of Service, and now make it possible for webmasters to insert a snippet of code to prevent their images from being pinned. However, I don't recommend you do it if you are on Pinterest specifically to market your business.

Lastly, Pinterest overhauled both its Terms of Service and its Copyright policy pages in response to outcry about the original policies. You can view each by visiting Pinterest and mousing over the About link, and choosing either Terms of Service or Copyright from the menu.

There's a common misconception that content on the web is all in the public domain. On the contrary, any content that's published should be assumed to be protected by copyright. It's allowable as "fair use," which allows for brief excerpts of content to be quoted, to use in a pin description a quote or short excerpt from someone else's copyrighted content. You can't, however, copy the bulk (or even a large portion) of the content.

A great resource on copyright law is the U.S. Copyright Office's site at `http://copyright.gov/`, which includes the entire U.S. copyright law, tip sheets, downloadable brochures, and an FAQ page.

Although there's no exact rule on a number of words or a percentage of content that defines fair use, a great guideline is to ask yourself whether someone would have to click through your pin to the original content to find out all they need to know. If they wouldn't need to click through — meaning your pin captures the entire essence of the post or the article — you've included too much information in your pin description.

The core issue that will probably need resolution in the near future is Pinterest's usage of full-size images on the pin pages themselves. The rest of Pinterest functions essentially as any other social bookmarking site, where a thumbnail and a snippet of an article is posted and you must click through to read the full content. This happens on Facebook, Google+, Digg, StumbleUpon, and several other sites.

What Pinterest does differently is to have a full-size image page when you visit a specific pin page. This could be something they ultimately need to change (perhaps to cap it to a specific maximum thumbnail size).

Regardless, I expect the copyright conversation about Pinterest is not over.

Chapter 2

Setting Up a Pinterest Account

In This Chapter

▶ Deciding whether to use a business or personal identity

▶ Getting an invitation

▶ Maintaining control of your business Pinterest account

▶ Understanding the etiquette and lingo

Setting up a Pinterest account isn't terribly difficult or time-consuming; later in this chapter, I show you how. You will want to get off on the right foot, however. To do so with a Pinterest profile geared at marketing, it is best to think through a few things beforehand. For example, will you set up as a human with a personal name that promotes and represents the business? If so, who will run the account? These are questions that are best resolved before you even click register.

Deciding Whether to Use a Business or Personal Identity

There is no crystal clear answer to the question about whether to be a logo or a face, I am afraid. There are pros and cons to using either. In a perfect situation, you would in fact have both. The business owner or social media manager or marketing director might have a personal account used for both their own stuff and sharing business-related pins, and the brand itself would have an official account that is solely dedicated to the business.

The standard for large businesses and brands, especially those that are household names, is to use the business name and logo when establishing a Pinterest account (as you can see in Figure 2-1, where Lindt Chocolate uses its name, profile image, and description for company references only). This is best for transparency's sake, even if for no other reason.

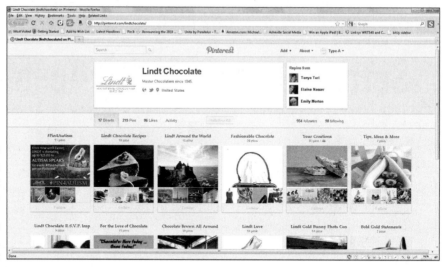

Figure 2-1:
Lindt
Chocolate
uses a
business
profile.

For smaller businesses and individual bloggers, writers and artists, the answer is less clear. In many cases, especially if people know you as an individual on other social networks, a personal account with your face could be the most engaging and effective option.

In personally experimenting with both personal and business accounts, I have found people are more likely to interact and engage with a human face profile than a brand logo profile, for example. Time may also be a factor. If you already have a personal account, adding a few boards is far less time consuming than adding and maintaining a second profile. Beyond the upkeep of maintaining both a business and personal account, if you have both, you will need to repeatedly log in to and out of your accounts in Pinterest.

You can still include your business information in your personal profile under your About section, as well as a link to your site. I describe how to set up your Pinterest profile in Chapter 3.

Having a personal account does not prevent you from promoting your business. You can create business-specific boards on a personal profile to get a mix of the benefits of both a personal account and a business one (see Figure 2-2).

For many businesses, however, a profile that is based on your brand name and logo makes the most sense. That is especially the case if you are joining Pinterest only for the purpose of establishing the business and marketing the business on Pinterest.

Figure 2-2:
A blogger
with a
personal
profile, but a
board
promoting
her blog
posts.

Here are some of the benefits of having a business-based profile on Pinterest:

✔ You get a boost in brand recognition, and it is much easier for existing fans and customers to find you. If your company is a popular brand or a household name, people will likely search out the company, so using that name increases your number of followers.

✔ If you inject some fun into your activity on Pinterest, using a brand name instead of a person's name allows you to humanize the brand.

✔ It is clearer for people following you, and there is no question that you are on Pinterest to represent the company.

✔ People expect a higher level of self-promotion from a business account. This doesn't give you a free pass to spam pin after pin about your business, but it does provide more leeway than a personal account.

For others, a personal account with some business-related boards makes more sense. This is particularly true if you already have built up a sizable, engaged personal profile elsewhere, or you have limited resources for staff to maintain it. For many small businesses, sole proprietorships and solo bloggers, a personal account with business-related boards makes the most sense.

A good guideline for deciding is this: Are *you* actually the brand or business? For bloggers, sole proprietors, and those who sell handmade goods or creations, people often associate the business so closely with the person that a business account with logo can be disconcerting.

Here are some benefits of using a personal profile on Pinterest:

- ✔ **People are more likely to engage with a person and a face than they are to engage with a business name and a logo.** In fact, I have heard people say they don't follow any businesses on Pinterest.

- ✔ **If you already have a personal account, it's less time-consuming to add boards to that than it is to juggle two Pinterest accounts.**

- ✔ **People trust a person more than a business.**

- ✔ **You have more freedom to post things not related to the business as well as those related to the business, as people expect a mix from a personal account.**

- ✔ **You won't be confined by topics only directly or indirectly related to your business.**

Another option if you already have a personal account is to start by creating a board or two that is specific to your business and experiment with it. See if you enjoy it or you have fun. Just keep in mind that if you decide to go with a separate business account later, there is no quick and easy way to transfer the boards to the new account (although you can repin the original pins to the new account).

Deciding Who Should Run Your Pinterest Account

If you are a freelancer, blogger, or an independent small business or professional, you are probably the best person to run your account. For a larger company or major brand, you will likely assign it to a staff member (or multiple staff members) or an outside firm.

Here are some of the options for selecting a person (or people) to run your Pinterest account:

- ✔ **Have the business owner or CEO run it:** The plus side of this option is that no one else knows the company or the brand as well as the owner or CEO does. The downside is the owner or CEO likely has little time to run it. If time and resources allow, letting the owner or CEO have a personal account plus having an official company account is ideal. For example, Maxine Clark of Build-a-Bear Workshop maintains her own account (see Figure 2-3).

  Meanwhile, the company itself also has a Pinterest profile (see Figure 2-4).

Figure 2-3:
Maxine
Clark,
founder
of Build-
A-Bear
Workshop,
maintains
a personal
Pinterest
account.

Figure 2-4:
The Build-
A-Bear
Workshop
official
Pinterest
profile.

✔ **Hire someone to run the Pinterest account.** This has the obvious benefit of freeing you from the time commitment, and if you select carefully to find someone who knows Pinterest inside and out, you get the benefits of someone who gets the space already. This is an option for both small and large businesses. If you already have a firm or consultant handling other social media accounts, it could be pretty seamless to add Pinterest. Having one agency in charge of it all should help you maintain consistent messaging. The downsides are that the consultant or firm likely won't understand the brand as well as someone in-house, and there is the added cost of outsourcing.

✔ **Assign a person or people from your in-house staff to handle the account.** If you have a social media manager, she is the obvious choice because she probably is already playing on Pinterest in her personal time and should have a great understanding of social media. You might need to train other staffers (for example, traditional public relations tactics and effective social media tactics are very different). You could give the staffer this book to help. The plus of this is the person or people handling it understand the business well. The downside is that it will take time and resources away from their other work tasks.

It can be tempting to use an intern or someone new to the company to run the Pinterest account (or other social media accounts). I would caution against that for a few reasons. Just as you wouldn't put an intern in charge of public relations duties or running a press conference, you don't want someone new and inexperienced in charge of your front line on the social web. There is also a myth that younger people are the only ones who "get" social media, but that simply isn't the case. In fact, on Pinterest, the demographics lean heavily towards members from their 30s through middle age.

Getting an Invitation to Join Pinterest

There are two methods of getting invited to Pinterest. One involves requesting an invitation directly from Pinterest and waiting for it to arrive. It typically takes a day or two, but sometimes it can take up to a couple of weeks. If you are the impatient type, you can also get in by having a current member send you an invitation.

Requesting an invitation on Pinterest is quite simple — just follow these steps:

1. **Click the large red Request an Invite button on the top-middle area on the Pinterest home page.**

   A form appears, as shown in Figure 2-5.

2. **Enter your e-mail address and click the Request Invitation button.**

   You are taken to a confirmation page and encouraged to browse pins while you wait for your invitation (see Figure 2-6). You'll receive a confirmation e-mail letting you know you're on the wait list. A formal invitation arrives in your inbox in about one to two days, typically.

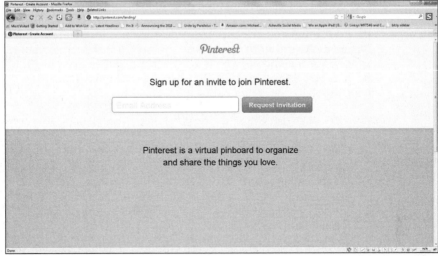

Figure 2-5:
Request
an invita-
tion from
Pinterest.

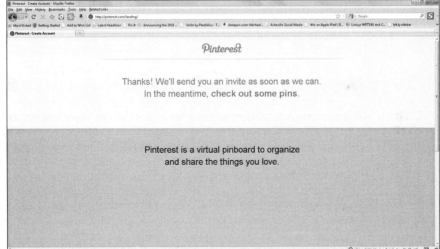

Figure 2-6:
Confir-
mation for
your invita-
tion request
at Pinterest.

If you don't receive the confirmation e-mail within minutes, check your
e-mail's spam folder. If the confirmation e-mail goes into spam, the
chances are good the actual invitation will land in the spam folder as
well, and you'll miss it. If the confirmation e-mail did land there, use your
e-mail provider's method for reporting that an e-mail is not spam.

The quicker and easier method of getting an invitation is to ask for one from a friend who's already a Pinterest member. The great advantage to this method is that you get instant gratification because you receive your invite immediately (rather than being on the wait list). The disadvantage is that you need to know someone who is a Pinterest member. That might not be as difficult as you think, however. Pinterest has millions of members, and many are happy to help newcomers join.

Here are a few ways to find a friend to ask to invite you:

- ✔ **Search for the keyword** Pinterest **on Twitter to see whether someone you know is a member already.** To do so, log in to Twitter and enter **Pinterest** as a search term in the top Search bar or visit `http://twitter.com/#!/search/pinterest`. The search results include anyone who has shared a pin on Twitter in a tweet as well as people who tweet about Pinterest.

- ✔ **Browse Pinterest.com to see whether someone already there is a friend of yours.** You can either visit the home page pins to see whether you recognize any names (a long shot) or type a name into the Search field in the top-left corner of the screen and click the magnifying glass. When you get the results, click the People filter link to view search results by users' names. If you see someone you already know, ask your friend for an invitation by email or messaging them however you usually communicate.

- ✔ **Check the Pinterest page on Facebook.** Go to `www.facebook.com/pinterest` and click the Like button if you haven't already. You see a list of your friends who are Pinterest fans (as shown in the bottom right of Figure 2-7). From there, you can message a friend (either through Facebook's private messaging on your friend's profile page or, if you know it, through the person's e-mail address) and ask for an invitation. You can also simply post a status update on Twitter, Google+, or Facebook that you're seeking an invitation to Pinterest. In many cases, you'll find that someone you know is already a member and is happy to extend an invitation.

When you've found a friend who is willing to invite you to Pinterest, give that friend your e-mail address. They can click the red Invite Friends button at the top right of the home page when they're logged in to Pinterest.

Figure 2-7:
The
Pinterest
Facebook
page show-
ing all
friends who
are fans of
Pinterest.

Maintaining Control of Your Pinterest Account

If you are running your account yourself for a small company you own, this isn't a big issue. For everyone else, especially large companies with typical staff turnaround and those who outsource their social media work, you must do a few things first before you start on Pinterest:

✔ **Make it very clear you are hiring the person or asking the staff member to use Pinterest on the company's behalf, and that the account will be owned and controlled by the company.** You do not want a profile to build a following and get wildly popular, and then have a staff member (or firm) get fired and take it with him or claim the account belongs to him.

✔ **Control access to the account by using a company-based e-mail for signup.** If you let someone use their own personal e-mail account to sign up, you will have no way to get back into the account if they quit or leave.

If you will have staff members or firms handling Pinterest or any social media accounts, consider creating a social media email in your business domain. Then if someone quits in a huff, gets fired, or simply is unreachable, you can easily get into that e-mail account to recover a password or change the profile.

✔ **Keep a master copy of the password and any other pertinent access details.** It is always a good idea to ensure anyone in the company can use the Pinterest account if need be. This can be especially important if your account is hacked and someone is sending out spam or inappropriate pins. This hasn't been reported as a major issue, but there have been isolated incidents of Pinterest account hacking. If the person who maintains the account is on an island vacation off the grid, you need to be sure someone can get into the account.

✔ **Be careful about whose Twitter and Facebook accounts are integrated into the Pinterest account.** If you have a business Twitter account to connect to your Pinterest profile, that is not as big of an issue. As of this writing, however, you can only integrate a personal Facebook account with Pinterest. Although there are many benefits to doing that, especially to gain followers (see Chapter 3), this hands over access to the staff member or firm representative whose personal Facebook profile is connected.

Setting Up Your New Account

After you receive your invitation, you notice you need either a Twitter or a Facebook account to complete your registration. If you don't already have a Twitter (`http://twitter.com`) or a Facebook (`http://facebook.com`) account, create one. You can get an account for free with either one, and you can set up an account with either very easily and quickly. You also need to activate the account or accounts before you can use them for your Pinterest registration.

If you must choose only one social network to integrate, note that Twitter is preferable for a business because you can connect it to a business Twitter account. Facebook has the advantage of pulling in all your friends on that network to allow you to easily add them as friends on Pinterest. Unless it is the personal account of the business owner, however, you may want to be careful about who integrates the personal account (see "Maintaining Control of Your Pinterest Account" in the previous section).

To integrate your Facebook or Twitter account with Pinterest, follow these steps:

1. **Log in to your Facebook or Twitter account.**

   Logging in isn't strictly necessary at this point, but doing so makes your registration go more smoothly. Keep in mind that this must be a Twitter or Facebook account not already integrated with Pinterest. If it is, it will log you into that Pinterest account instead of completing your new registration.

2. In the Pinterest invitation e-mail you received, click the link to register.

The Pinterest registration screen appears, as shown in Figure 2-8.

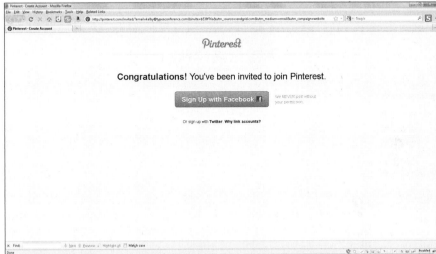

Figure 2-8:
The
Pinterest
registra-
tion screen
asks you
sign up via
Facebook or
Twitter.

3. Click either the Facebook button or the Twitter link.

You can add either one at registration and then integrate the other one later if you choose.

4. Enter your profile details in the text boxes provided.

You're prompted for three basic profile details, as shown in Figure 2-9:

- Your username
- Your e-mail address
- Your password

Choose your username carefully. It determines the URL for your pro-file on Pinterest. (For example, mine is http://www.pinterest.com/typeacon.) Pinterest recently added the option to change your user-name — however, it's not ideal to do so because any existing links to your profile will no longer work.

5. Click the Create Account button.

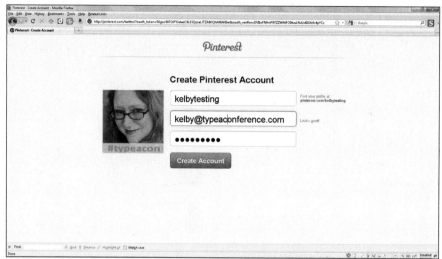

Figure 2-9:
Create your
Pinterest
profile.

You're officially a member of Pinterest — congratulations! Continue reading the next section to find out how to complete the setup of your new Pinterest profile.

Setting up your profile

After you've integrated Pinterest with your Facebook or Twitter account (see the previous section), you must go through a few steps to set up your basic Pinterest profile. This profile takes only a few seconds to complete. When you're finished, you'll be following some Pinterest members, and you'll see pins in your stream.

Some of these options appear only during the registration process (such as the suggested followers), so be aware you won't be able to return to all of these steps. To begin setting up your profile, follow these steps:

1. **Indicate your interests by clicking the images for any that apply.**

   Figure 2-10 shows the Interests page with a few items already selected. This can be a chance to follow some people with similar interests as soon as you join. As you click each interest, the image turns green to indicate it has been selected. You can deselect by clicking a topic image a second time.

   Although Pinterest tells you it's going to suggest a few members for you to follow, this statement is a little misleading. In actuality, Pinterest automatically sets up your account to follow a few members who match your interests. (If you don't want to follow these members, no problem — you can unfollow them right away as I describe in the next step.)

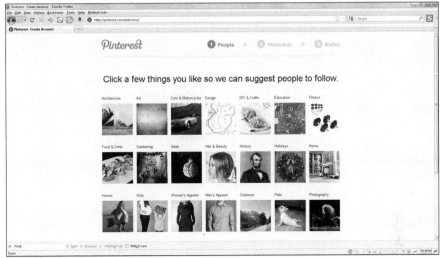

Figure 2-10:
Choose
interests
during pro-
file set-up.

2. **Click the Follow People button at the bottom of the page (you may need to scroll down to view the button).**

3. **Review the members you're now following and make any necessary adjustments.**

   After you indicate your interests, Pinterest displays the list of members it has chosen for you to follow. (See Figure 2-11.) At this stage, you can click the Unfollow button to remove anyone you don't want to follow from this list.

4. **Click the Create Boards button.**

   The Create Your First Pinboards page appears, as seen in Figure 2-12.

5. **Name your new pinboards by using the appropriate text boxes.**

   Your profile and pins are organized by these boards. Pinterest automatically suggests some boards for you to create, such as Products I Love, Favorite Places & Spaces, and Books Worth Reading. You can use those, or you can change the text in the boxes to boards you would like to create. To delete a suggested board, mouse over the right side of the box. Click the X that appears in the bottom-right corner of any board name to remove that board.

   You don't need to agonize over boards as you go through this process. You can easily create more boards later. (I cover creating boards in detail in Chapter 4.) You can also edit the name and description of a board at any time.

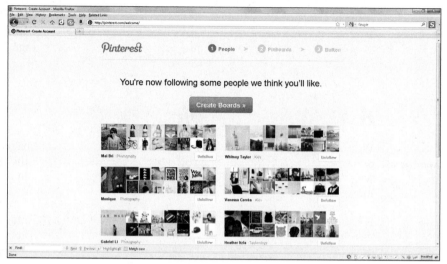

Figure 2-11:
See who
Pinterest
followed for
your profile.

Figure 2-12:
Create your
first
pinboards.

6. (Optional) Add the Pin It bookmark button.

Pinterest prompts you to do this now, but you don't have to. You can wait until I cover this process in detail in Chapter 4. Depending on your browser, this step shows instructions on adding a Pin It button. In most browsers, you drag the button on the screen up to your browser's top toolbar.

7. **Click the Start Pinning button (you may have to scroll down to see it).**

   Your personal profile appears. From here, you can start pinning things. To get started, click the Pinterest logo at the top of the page to see what other have pinned. If you like something you see, repin it!

Adding a profile picture

When you signed up, Pinterest acquired your default profile image (or *avatar*) automatically — it copied the profile image you were using at the social network that you integrated during registration. If you like, you can change that image at any time.

Having a profile picture is a must-do on most social networks, and this is the case with Pinterest. People tend to ignore, not follow, and not interact with members who have no avatar. If you are creating a business profile, a logo or image of a product works well. If you are creating a personal profile, a close-up headshot is ideal. Cartoon characters, pets (unless your business is pet-related), and children's faces instead of your own can be off-putting to other members who are looking to engage with either you or your brand.

To change your profile picture, log in to Pinterest, mouse over your name in the top-right corner of the Pinterest home page, and choose Settings from the drop-down menu. When the Settings page appears, scroll down a bit to see your Image options, as shown in Figure 2-13.

Figure 2-13:
Update your profile picture.

Depending on which platform you chose to integrate your Pinterest account with (either Facebook or Twitter), you have up to three choices:

- ✔ **Upload an Image:** To upload an image from your computer, click this button. The button changes instantly to a text field and a Browse button. Click the Browse button to open the Choose File to Upload dialog box. Then navigate through your files to seek out your image, select it, and click the Open button to upload it to Pinterest.

- ✔ **Refresh from Facebook:** If you have an updated image from Facebook you would like to use, click this button. This option appears only if you have Facebook integrated with your Pinterest account.

- ✔ **Refresh from Twitter:** Like the Facebook button, this button changes your profile image to the one you're currently using on Twitter. This option appears only if you have Twitter integrated with your Pinterest account.

An ideal profile image is square. Also, it must at least be 200x200 pixels in size, or it will appear pixelated and distorted on your profile page.

Adding a bio

A bio helps tell others on Pinterest about you. When someone visits your profile page, your bio is displayed just below your profile picture in the left column.

To update your bio, log in to Pinterest, mouse over your name in the top-right corner of the home page, and choose Settings from the drop-down menu. (You can also find it by clicking your name or visiting your main profile page and clicking the Edit Profile link right under your bio at the top center.) To update your bio, adjust the About section of the resulting form accordingly, as shown in Figure 2-14. On this form, you can also update various other personal details such as your name, location, and website.

The bio is text only. You can't use HTML coding in your bio to, say, place sections in boldface or to add a link to your site. Any HTML code will be displayed, not rendered, and if you include a full URL, it won't be made into a clickable link. You can, however, include a linkable web page or blog URL in the Website field in Settings. (See Figure 2-14.)

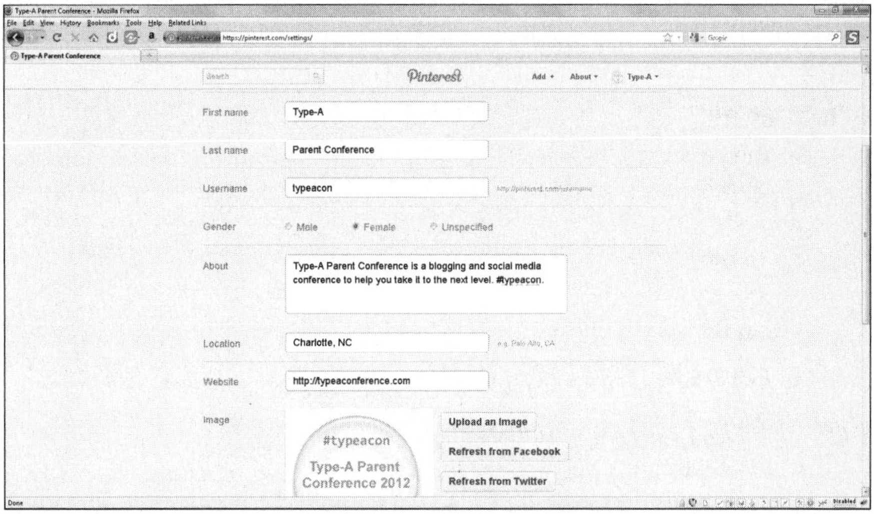

Figure 2-14:
Enter your
bio on
Pinterest.

Setting your e-mail preferences

Do you want Pinterest to notify you of all activity related to your profile by
e-mail alert? Or do you dislike e-mails and prefer to get your updates when
you go directly to the site? The Pinterest settings allow for a variety of preferences. Figure 2-15 shows a list of options you can choose to refine your
updates; you access this list by clicking Settings and then clicking Change
E-mail Settings (found next to the Notifications header).

Figure 2-15:
E-mail
preferences
in Pinterest.

E-mail alerts are handy for keeping track of activity, such as when people repin (or share) your pins, follow you, or comment on your pins. At the time of this writing, though, the e-mail alerts are spotty. Pinterest is a new site, and glitches are to be expected. Don't rely only on e-mail notifications — check Pinterest as well. To access your updates at Pinterest, mouse over your name and choose Pins from the drop-down menu to see the number of repins, likes, and comments for your latest pins. Pinterest also shows the latest activity in the left column on the home page when you're logged in. For more detail on a particular pin, click its thumbnail to navigate to the pin page.

Understanding the Social Etiquette for Businesses on Pinterest

On every social network, like in life, no one likes people who only talk about themselves. All the time. This is just as true on Pinterest as other sites, and perhaps even more so. Many members have come to view Pinterest as a place of beauty and inspiration. Spam and excessive self-promotion is viewed harshly by the community.

Still, if you want to market on Pinterest, you can't exist as a martyr on the site, right? There is no doubt that people are self-promoting there. What you want to avoid, just as you would in a real-life conversation, is overdoing it. Share a little about yourself, and then share other members' content and pins.

Here are some general guidelines to following Pinterest etiquette:

- **Don't just hoard followers, but follow people back.** This is, I believe, especially true if your purpose is marketing. No one likes to feel snubbed. When a member sees a favorite brand is followed by a million but is only following ten people, they get irritated.

- **Share about others more than you share about your company.** Yes, of course, if you have a great post or an exciting new product, pin it. But you should follow an 80-20 rule: Make sure no more than one in five pins is self-promotional. You can share less about yourself than that, but don't share more. Don't be that guy at the party that everyone avoids.

- **Pin images from their original source and credit properly.** A big source of the copyright controversy and issues is related to people pinning images from places that are not the source (Google image search and Tumblr, for example). Avoid creating original pins that don't properly connect to the source, and also avoid repinning poorly sourced pins. You can always click through a pin to see where the original pin leads before you repin. I cover more about how to pin properly in Chapter 4.

Pinterest's own etiquette recommendations, in fact, removed a statement to avoid self-promotion. I wouldn't take that as a free pass, but an indication that they realize many businesses have discovered the power of Pinterest and are using it to drive awareness and traffic.

You can also find Pinterest's own etiquette recommendations by clicking About in the top toolbar, and then clicking Pin Etiquette in the left column that appears (see Figure 2-16).

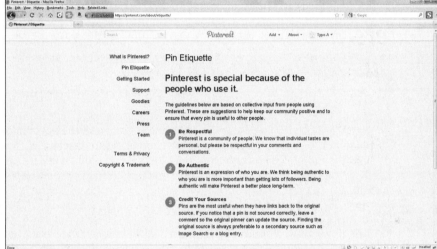

Figure 2-16:
Pinterest has its own etiquette recommendations.

Understanding the Pinterest Lingo

Before we dive into using Pinterest in the next chapter, it can be helpful to understand the various terms you will encounter on Pinterest, in articles about Pinterest, and in conversations about Pinterest. These terms come up repeatedly in this book, so it's a good idea to become familiar with them:

- ✔ **Pinboard:** A group of pins organized on your Pinterest profile by a topic set by you. They are also called "boards."

- ✔ **Pin:** As a verb, it is to share an image on a pinboard. By pinning an image you either upload or find on the web, it will appear on your Pins page, in the stream of those who follow you, and on your board page. As a noun, it is an image you have shared on Pinterest.

✔ **Repin:** When you see another member's pin that you like, you can add it to one of your own boards and share it with your own followers by clicking Repin. It is similar to a retweet on Twitter.

✔ **Like:** When you see another member's pin you like, you can click Like to indicate it. This places you on a list of people who like the pin on the pin's page, and it shows this pin on your personal profile's Likes page. Liking an image does not repin the image — it won't show up in one of your pinboards.

✔ **Hashtag:** You can include a tag in a pin's description by prepending a word with the number sign using the format #keyword (no spaces or other characters). When you do this, the word becomes clickable. Clicking it takes users to search results for that term.

✔ **Follower:** On your profile, your list of followers includes people who follow all of your boards.

✔ **Following:** On your profile, your following list includes the profiles for which you are following all boards.

✔ **Mention:** When you are following someone and they are following you back in return, you can mention them in a pin description by typing the @ symbol. This brings up a pull-down list as you type a member's name. When done, the name becomes linkable to the person's profile.

✔ **Pin It Button:** This is a browser add-on that allows you to pin an image directly from the web page where you found it.

✔ **Pin It Button for Web:** This is a button you can place on your own web site or blog to allow people to pin an image directly from your site with a click of the button. (I have instructions for this in Chapter 9.)

Chapter 3

Following People on Pinterest

In This Chapter

▶ Tips for finding people to follow on Pinterest

▶ Finding Facebook friends to follow

▶ Finding e-mail contacts to follow

▶ Finding your target customers to follow

*P*interest can be pretty quiet without friends. It isn't a race to see who can collect the most friends, but you will need a certain number in order to engage and interact well.

For example, as you add followers, your home page (which is a stream of the latest pins and repins from the people you follow) becomes an interesting, diverse, and fun place to visit. It will also give you a better choice of pins to repin, like, and comment on.

People also tend to follow members who are following them (although following someone is not a guarantee they will return the favor). Many members have e-mail notifications set up so they're alerted when they get new followers, and their home page displays their recent followers.

When you signed up, Pinterest should have automatically followed some members according to the interests you indicated (previously covered in Chapter 2). You can also tie Facebook, Yahoo! Mail, and Gmail into your account to add your friends and contacts, which I cover later in this chapter.

If you choose Follow All (meaning you want to follow all of their Pinterest boards) when following new people on Pinterest, your profile appears in their list of followers and you are included in their follower count. If you instead choose to follow select boards only, you don't appear in their profile's follower list. I recommend using Follow All for a few reasons, including being a better community member as well as encouraging people to follow your profile by being more visible. If a member has a lot of pins to an individual board that annoy you or simply don't interest you, you can later unfollow single boards. This keeps you in their profile's list of followers, but pins from that board won't show in your home page stream of pins.

Companies and web sites are popping up with offers to help you buy followers and repins, or offering webinars on how to gain thousands of followers overnight. Avoid these offers. A quality Pinterest consultant or trainer knows that gaining traction on Pinterest is about much more than collecting followers and does not happen overnight. Be wary of anyone who promises easy and overnight success (usually for a price). Concentrate on building a following of people who are engaged and interested in your business — that takes time and effort spent being active on Pinterest.

Using Pinterest Site and Search to Find People to Follow

A great place to start seeking out friends is to poke around the Pinterest site. There are four primary methods of finding people to follow using the Pinterest site alone (without even integrating third-party sites). They include

- Use Pinterest search
- Use Pinterest categories and most popular pins
- Use the Pinterest Everything stream
- See who your friends are following and who is following them

I explain each of these methods in the coming sections.

Using Pinterest search to find people to follow

The Pinterest search allows you to search individual pins, board names, and member names. This means you can find people who share pins and create boards on various topics, and you can find people you know by doing name searches for members.

Search is a great way to find people to follow who are sharing pins or have created boards on topics related to your business. Brainstorm several search terms for ideas for your business and a potential friend's shared interests. The searches can be general (such as crafts) or specific (such as jewelry-making).

You can use the search to find people through three methods. Each time you search, the default is for the results to be from pins. You can also click Boards at the top to switch to a search of board names, or you can click People to apply the search term to profile names. This three-tiered search provides great options for finding people to follow.

To use Pinterest search to find people to follow by search, follow these steps:

1. **Type a search term or phrase in the Search box found in the top left corner of any Pinterest page, and then click the magnifying glass icon to run the search (as seen in Figure 3-1).**

Figure 3-1:
The Search box at the top left of Pinterest's home page.

The search results page appears, which defaults to results of Pin searches. You can opt to see pin results, or you can click Boards or People to change the search filter.

REMEMBER

If you type the first few letters of the name of someone you already follow, their profile appears as a drop-down. You can click the name and go to their boards, or ignore it and continue typing your search term.

2. **Browse the pins to find ones that interest you and find the person who pinned it.**

Each pin on the search results page has a gray box listing who pinned it and what board they pinned it to. Look for *(member name)* onto *(board name.)*

3. **Mouse over the person's name and you will see it becomes an underlined, clickable link (see Figure 3-2).**

Click the name to visit the person's profile page.

4. **Click the red Follow All button at the top center, as you can see in Figure 3-3 below the member's photo and description.**

Figure 3-2:
Each pin image lists the person's name, which is a clickable link.

The clickable link

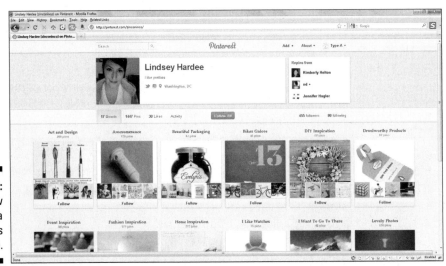

Figure 3-3:
Click Follow All on a member's profile page.

Pinterest limits the number of people you can follow to ensure a spammer or bot doesn't register and follow thousands of members all at once. Although Pinterest hasn't officially announced a cap, my testing shows that you are limited to following no more than three times the number of members who follow you. For example, if you have 1,000 followers, you can follow no more than 3,000 members. This might sound limiting, but honestly, people get just as suspicious of members with a high following-to-follower ratio as they do members with a high follower-to-following ratio.

Another great tactic for finding people to follow is to find people who have created boards with keywords related to your business. This is useful because you know these are Pinterest members who are interested enough in a topic to dedicate a board to the subject, whereas an individual pin could be the only time someone shared on that topic. This is a powerful way to find and connect with people passionate about the same topics your business relates to.

To use Pinterest search to find people to follow via certain board topics, follow these steps:

1. **While logged into Pinterest, find the Search box at the top left.**

   Type a search term, and then click the magnifying glass icon to run the search. This takes you to the search results page, which defaults to results of pin searches.

2. **Click Boards to filter the results so they only show boards with the search term in the name.**

   You can find the Boards link to filter your results at the top left of the page (see Figure 3-4).

3. **Browse the boards to find members you want to follow.**

   Just below each board name is the name of the member who created it. Click the name (each name is linkable and turns red when you mouse over it).

4. **Click the red Follow All button just below the member's picture and description.**

Figure 3-4:
Filtering
the search
results
to show
boards with
your search
phrase.

Finally, you can use Pinterest search to find members by name. This can be helpful to find people you personally know, other companies you want to follow, or bloggers and social media influencers who write about topics related to your business.

To use the people search on Pinterest:

1. **While logged into Pinterest, find the Search box at the top left.**

   Type a search term, and then click the magnifying glass icon to run the search. This takes you to the search results page, which defaults to results of pin searches.

2. **Click People to filter the results so they only show boards with the search term in the name.**

   The People link to filter your results is at the top left of the page.

   The people search on Pinterest searches both the member's name and their username. For example, my member name for my business page is Type-A Parent Conference, but my username is *typeacon*. You can search either "type-a parent" or "typeacon" and find my profile in the results. This means if you are, for example, searching for a blogger to follow, you might find them by searching for their name, their blog name, or their commonly used username or handle on sites such as Twitter. For a personal account, people might use their real name and use a common online handle for their username. For a business account, you could have all business name references or a business owner's human name followed by a username that is their business name, for example.

3. **Browse the results to find members to follow, and click the Follow button below members' pictures (as seen in Figure 3-5).**

   Alternately, you can click their profile picture to be taken to their full profile page to see what kinds of boards they have and whether the member is active before deciding to follow.

Using Pinterest categories and Popular pins to find people to follow

Another great tactic for finding new people to follow is to use Pinterest's categories and Popular pin pages to find kindred spirits and members who spark engagement to follow. Pinterest has several categories covering everything from art and geek to kids and sports.

To find people through category pages, be sure you're logged in to Pinterest, and then follow these steps:

1. **Mouse over the Everything link at the top of the page.**

   A drop-down menu with a list of the various categories appears, as seen at the top of Figure 3-6.

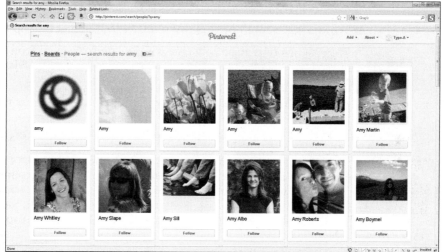

Figure 3-5:
Click the
Follow
button
under a
profile
picture
when doing
a people
search.

Figure 3-6:
Finding the
Pinterest
categories.

2. **Find a category that interests you and click the name in the drop-down menu.**

   Each board created on Pinterest is part of a category. The category page shows you pins that are on boards in that category, as seen in Figure 3-7. Notice that the top menu changes from Everything to text that states Everything: *Category Name* (in this case, Pets).

3. **Browse the pins to find people whose pins interest you.**

   Right below the pin image and description (and under the number of repins and likes), click the member's name to visit their profile page.

4. **On the profile page, click the red Follow All button or choose to follow individual boards.**

You can also use the Popular link at the top of the Pinterest homepage to find people to follow. Although Pinterest hasn't gone on record stating what exactly makes a pin land on the Popular page, I suspect it's a mix of number of repins, likes, and comments.

What is interesting is that Pinterest is a true level playing field. Notice as you visit the Popular page that many of the pins originated with members who don't have many followers.

Unlike many other social networks, where the highest level of sharing often comes from members with huge followings, the popularity of a pin on Pinterest depends heavily on how interesting and viral the image is, not how many followers a person has.

Category name

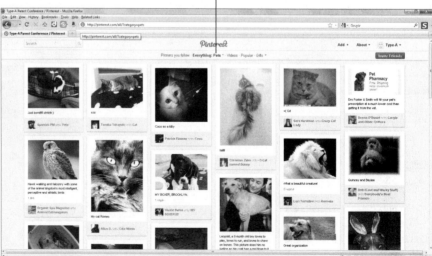

Figure 3-7:
A category
pin result
page.

Still, you can find members who clearly have engagement on Pinterest and who have a knack for pinning images that are popular. Although we cover repinning in Chapter 5, the Popular page can be a great place to find pins to repin. Because they are already popular, these pins have been vetted in a sense. I've found that the pins I repin from the Popular pin list get great response and engagement.

To find people to follow from the Popular page, follow these steps:

1. **From the home page, click Popular in the menu (as seen at the top center in Figure 3-8).**

2. **On the Popular page, browse pins to find people to follow.**

   You see the name of the pinner below the pin image, description, and statistics (repins and likes).

3. **Click the names of any members who interest you.**

   This takes you to their profile page, where you can click the red Follow All button to follow all their boards, or you can follow individual boards.

Using Pinterest Everything stream to find people to follow

You can visit the Everything stream to find people to follow as well. This is a much more random approach, but you may be surprised how quickly you find interesting pins that lead to interesting people.

Figure 3-8:
Click
Popular
from the
home page.

The bonus of using this tactic is that you are more likely to discover people (and those who pin on various topics) that could be great to follow but whom you may not have found in searches.

To follow people through the Everything page:

1. **While logged in, go to the Pinterest homepage and click Everything.**

   It is a text menu link located at the top center of the page.

2. **On the Everything page, browse to find pins that are interesting.**

   As you might expect and can see in Figure 3-9, the Everything page is a wildly diverse mix of pins. Still, when you browse, you will likely find some of interest quickly.

   If you go to the bottom of the results page, it will automatically load more pins. You can continue to do this to get more results.

3. **Directly below any image, description, and pin statistics, click the name of the person who created the pin.**

   Their profile page appears.

4. **Click the Follow All button at the top center, directly below the member's picture and description.**

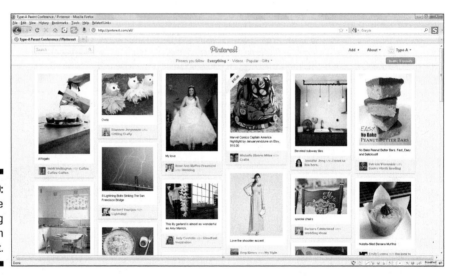

Figure 3-9:
The
Everything
page on
Pinterest.

Using Pinterest Friend and Follower lists to find people

You can also find friends by looking at the list of people who follow your existing friends or who your friends follow.

To follow your existing friends' followers and people they follow:

1. **While logged in, go to the home page and click your name at the top right corner.**

   It displays your name and a small profile avatar.

   Your profile page appears.

2. **You can click either Followers (to see members following your profile) or Following (to see a list of members you follow).**

   Followers and Following are text links towards the top right of the page, as shown in Figure 3-10. You can also go through these steps here for one, and then repeat for the other.

   When you click either link, you arrive at a page with a list of members.

Followers / Following links

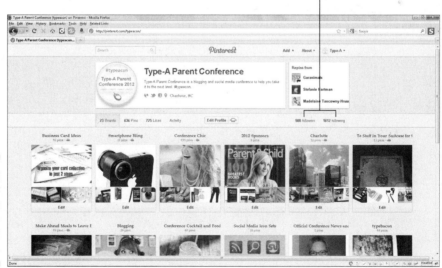

Figure 3-10: Finding your followers and people following you.

3. **Click any name to the right of a member's profile (see Figure 3-11).**

   This takes you to their profile page.

4. **From there, click that member's Followers or Following page (with the same method as in Step 2).**

   This takes you to the page with a list of either followers or members following them.

5. **Click the Follow All button to the right of each profile (see Figure 3-12) for any member you want to follow.**

Following your followers back

A quick and easy place to find people to follow is to simply see who is following your profile. Even if you are following more people than you have following you, the odds are good you're not following all of them.

People like to feel social network relationships are reciprocal. This is why "social" is right in the name. One of the most common mistakes I see brands, businesses, and organizations make on social networks (and Pinterest) is to follow very few of their fans back. As you can imagine, it is insulting to many members of the community. It also backfires, as some people look at a member's follower-to-following ratio before deciding whether to follow. If they see you follow only a tiny percentage of your followers, they may just keep on clicking away from your profile.

Figure 3-11:
The
Followers
page.

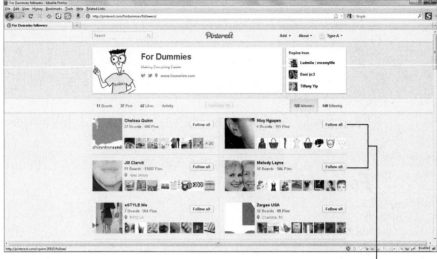

Figure 3-12:
The Follow
All button
on a list of
a member's
followers.

Follow All buttons

To see who is following you and follow them in return, use these steps:

1. **In the top menu, click your name at the top right corner.**

   You arrive at your profile page.

2. **Click the Followers text link to the top right of the page.**

   This takes you to a list of people following you. Some members in the list have a Follow All button and some have a button with faded text that says Unfollow (see Figure 3-13). If it says Follow All, you are not currently following the user. If it says Unfollow, you are following the member.

3. **Click the Follow All button for any member you want to follow.**

   If you have more followers than load at once, you can scroll to the bottom to fetch more members. Repeat to follow any members you wish. While you are on the page, if you see any member you want to unfollow, you can also do that by clicking the Unfollow button next to their profile in the list.

Figure 3-13:
Finding fol-
lowers who
you are not
following.

Finding Facebook Friends to Follow

The easiest, best, and fastest way to find people you know on Pinterest is to integrate Facebook into your account and find your Facebook friends who are already on Pinterest.

The downside of this for a business profile is that you need a human with a personal profile to use to do this. At the time of this writing, you cannot integrate Facebook business pages, for example, and find your business' fans. You also cannot find Twitter followers who are on Pinterest, which might allow you to find your Twitter business account's followers on Pinterest.

You can always use a personal Facebook account to follow all of your friends and then remove the Facebook account right afterwards if you prefer to avoid having the personal and business accounts mingling. I also have a trick for get-ting around Pinterest's limit to using one Facebook account on one Pinterest profile (see later in this section for instructions).

Although the steps below allow you to also invite all of your Facebook friends who are not currently on Pinterest in one click, I recommend against that. Many people don't like mass invitations to join new sites. A better method would be to individually invite Facebook friends who aren't yet on Pinterest when you get to Step 4 in the instructions below. You can also post an update on your Facebook personal profile or your business page to see if any of your friends or fans would like an invitation to Pinterest.

To find Facebook friends to follow on Pinterest:

1. **While logged in go to the homepage, mouse over your name at the top right and click Find Friends in the dropdown menu.**

   This will take you to the Find Friends page, where you by default see the Facebook friends options.

2. **If you haven't integrated Facebook yet, click the large Find Friends from Facebook button (as shown in Figure 3-14) — if you have Facebook already integrated, skip to Step 4.**

   This pops up a window from Facebook where, when logged into Facebook, you can see a Facebook app authorization (see Figure 3-15). If you would like, you can adjust who can see Pinterest updates on Facebook at the bottom left of the authorization by clicking the Friends drop-down menu and choosing who can see your updates.

3. **Click the blue Go to App button at the top right.**

   You return to the Pinterest Find Friends page. Allow it a moment to load your Facebook friends into the page.

4. **To the right of the page, you can click Follow All to follow all of your Facebook friends who are on Pinterest or you can individually click the Follow button (see Figure 3-16).**

Figure 3-14:
Click the
Find Friends
from
Facebook
button.

Figure 3-15:
The
Facebook
authoriza-
tion for the
Pinterest
app.

Figure 3-16:
Following
your
Facebook
friends on
Pinterest.

5. If you click Follow All, wait a moment.

It is subtle, but the site is following members. You will see a dot bouncing to the right of the Follow All button (see Figure 3-17). It is complete
when that stops.

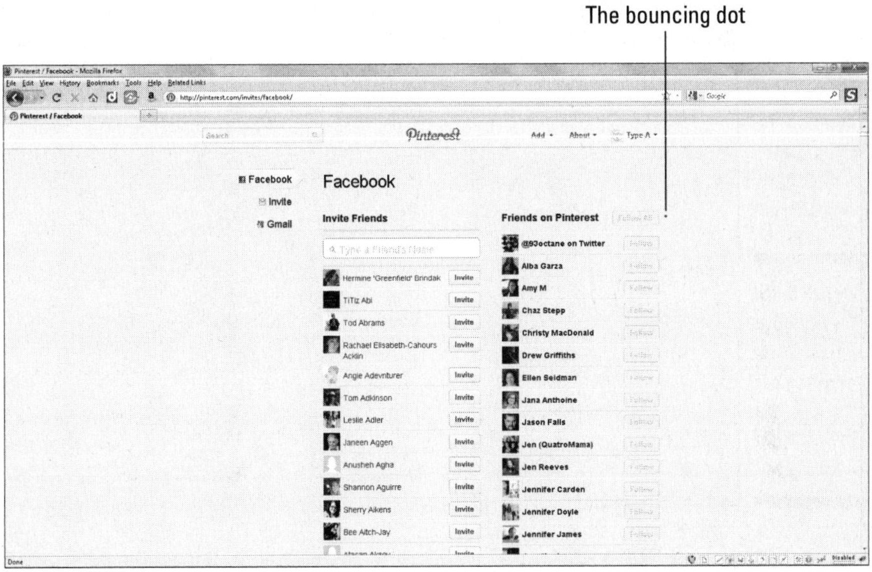

The bouncing dot

Figure 3-17:
Waiting for
Pinterest to
follow all of
your friends.

6. Refresh the web page to be sure all of the Facebook friends were in the first list if you are following all.

The Follow All button only follows friends listed on the page when you clicked it. Refresh your screen until you no longer see new Facebook friends appear if you want to truly follow all friends on Facebook.

If there are more to follow, new names later in the alphabet will appear. You can click Follow All again to follow these friends. If you exceed your following limit, you will see a pop-up box that reads Oops! Could Not Follow All Friends (see Figure 3-18). If that happens, you need to get more followers before you can follow new people.

Although Pinterest only allows you to connect your Facebook account to one Pinterest account, I discovered a simple workaround to that issue. You can remove a personal Facebook account from a personal Pinterest account, for instance, add it to a business Pinterest account, add Facebook friends there, and then restore it back to your personal account.

In essence, your Facebook account is only integrated with one Pinterest account at a time, but you could get the benefits in more than one Pinterest account.

Figure 3-18:
If you follow
too many
people
at once,
you are
restricted
from fol-
lowing new
people until
you get
more
followers.

If you are in the habit of logging into your account via Facebook log in instead of using your Pinterest user name/email address and password, you may not even remember your Pinterest password. If that is the case, before disconnecting the Facebook account, be sure to change your password to something you will remember. You can do that between Step 1 and Step 2 in the instructions below by clicking the Change Password button.

To use one Facebook account on multiple Pinterest profiles:

1. **Log in to the Pinterest account that is currently integrated with your Facebook personal profile.**

2. **Mouse over your profile name on the top right, and click Settings.**

   This takes you to the Edit Profile page with various options for your account.

3. **Scroll down until you see Facebook to the left, an On/Off toggle button, and Link to Facebook on the right (see Figure 3-19).**

4. **Click the toggle to Off, scroll down, and click the Save Profile button.**

5. **Mouse over your name at the top right of the site and click Log Out.**

6. **Log into the second Pinterest account.**

7. **Mouse over your profile name on the top right and click Settings.**

   Find the On/Off toggle switch on this profile and click On. This opens a pop-up box with the Facebook authorization (refer to Figure 3-15 earlier in this chapter).

Figure 3-19:
The Link to
Facebook
On/Off
switch.

8. **Click the Go to App button at the top right.**

You're returned to the Pinterest Edit Profile page.

9. **Click the Save Profile Button.**

From this point, you can follow the previous instructions to find Facebook friends to follow. You can follow all of the previous instructions again to disconnect from your second Pinterest profile and reconnect to your first profile again.

You can remove the Facebook integration from your business account immediately, and I would recommend that in the case of an employee or consultant/firm running a Pinterest account for a business, for example. If you are running both your own personal account (on Pinterest and Facebook) and your business Pinterest account, however, you might consider leaving it attached to your business account for a while. Members of Pinterest regularly visit the Find Friends page to find Facebook friends, and those friends will see whichever account you have connected to Facebook.

Finding E-mail Contacts to Follow

If you use Gmail or Yahoo! Mail for email, you can search for contacts who are already on Pinterest and follow them.

As I mentioned earlier for Facebook, you can also click Invite All to send an invitation to Pinterest to all of your Yahoo! or Gmail contacts who are not yet a member. I would, however, recommend against a mass invitation because it tends to irritate people. You can instead individually click Invite for Gmail or Yahoo! contacts one at a time.

To find Gmail contacts on Pinterest to follow:

1. **At the top right of the top menu, mouse over your name and click Find Friends in the drop-down menu.**

   The Find Friends page appears. By default, the Facebook option is selected.

2. **Click the Gmail or Yahoo! option in the right column.**

3. **Click the blue Find Friends from Gmail or Find Friends from Yahoo! button (as shown in Figure 3-20).**

   This prompts a popup to sign into Gmail or Yahoo! and asks permission for Pinterest to use the mail system. If you are already logged in, it simply reverts back to the Pinterest page after your authorization.

   Unlike the Facebook integration to find friends earlier in this chapter, you must re-authorize Gmail and Yahoo! every time you follow this process. The contact authorization is temporary and one-time, whereas the Facebook authorization remains until you remove it.

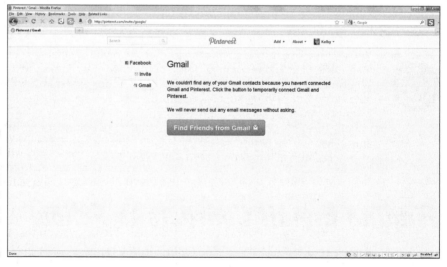

Figure 3-20:
Finding
e-mail
contacts
who are
members of
Pinterest.

4. **Click Follow All (as seen in the top right of Figure 3-21) or individually click Follow one by one.**

   For Follow All, you need to wait while a dot bounces up and down to the right of the Follow All button. Refresh the page to see if there are more contacts to follow.

Figure 3-21:
Following
your e-mail
contacts
who are on
Pinterest.

More Tips on Finding People to Follow

Although this chapter covers the key methods for finding people to follow on Pinterest, it is by no means a comprehensive list. Here are more creative ways to find great members to follow.

✔ **Search social networks for Pinterest talk.** Sometimes, simply searching on sites like Twitter for the keyword *Pinterest* can show you who is pinning and talking about Pinterest. In some cases, you will find people sharing their pins. Clicking those links takes you to the pin page, where you can find the linkable name of the person who pinned to click through and follow the member.

✔ **Check blog sidebars and company websites.** Many bloggers and companies now have anything from a small "P" square icon that is sometimes Pinterest red and sometimes the color of the website (such as in Figure 3-22) to a larger Follow Me on Pinterest button. Some websites even have widgets with the latest pins.

The Pinterest icon on a blog

Figure 3-22:
A Pinterest
icon on a
blog.

✔ **Search for profile linkups or weekly Pinterest linky posts.** For example, I have a linkup with hundreds of profiles of Pinterest members you can follow at `http://typeaparent.com/pinterest-profile-linkup.html`. You can also search terms like *Pinterest linkup* and *Pinterest linky* on Google.

✔ **Find top Pinterest profile lists and articles.** Zoomsphere (`www.zoomsphere.com/charts/pinterest/`) is a great resource for finding the most followed Pinterest members. Mashable (`http://Mashable.com`) also is a good resource and has regular top profile list posts. Just keep in mind that some of the members with the most followers, although extremely influential if they follow you back, are not likely to follow you back. You can look at a member's follower-to-following ratio to see how often they reciprocate follows.

Chapter 4

Creating Boards and Pins

In This Chapter

▶ Jumping into creating boards

▶ Interacting with collaborative boards

▶ Tweaking the appearance of your board

*T*he soul of Pinterest is in its pins and boards. This is where you show off your brand or business personality. The boards are a chance to showcase your interests and find people who are passionate about the same topics. Boards are also opportunities to get creative with fun and engaging names.

Creating Boards

You may have created some boards when you registered, but that was on the fly and before you dipped your toes into Pinterest. Now is the time to think through boards that are both engaging with members and a great tie-in for your organization.

Before you create a new board, consider a few things:

✔ **What interests you?** If you (or whoever is managing the Pinterest account for your company) don't find a board topic interesting, it will be tough to find pins and put much energy into that board.

✔ **What interests your customers, clients, or audience?** Sometimes this isn't exactly a topic related to your product, for example, but maybe an indirectly related topic. For example, Scholastic's profile has a board dedicated to book-related party ideas. That of course isn't tied directly to their products, but certainly anyone interested in reading (or passionate about books) would enjoy that creative and clever idea for a board.

✔ **Will your board topic be general or specific?** Either choice is perfectly acceptable, and odds are good you will eventually end up with a mix of some that are rather wide-ranging and some that are very targeted. In the beginning, broader board topics might be easier because more images can be pinned to it. For example, Betty Crocker has boards that are very general in relation to recipes, such as a cookie board and a cake board. They also have a couple that are very specific, such as Whoopie Pies (see Figure 4-1) and Game Day.

✔ **Will you have enough to pin to have a board with depth?** People don't like to follow a board with just a couple of pins, and sometimes get turned off from following a member who has boards with few or no pins. Before you start a board, be sure you can immediately populate it with at least five pins. That way, all thumbnails are filled out on your profile board page. Lance Crackers, for example, created a new profile and has a couple boards without enough pins to populate the thumbnail spots on the profile (as you can see on the two boards to the right of Figure 4-2). Also be sure you will have enough content to pin or repin to keep the board going over time.

✔ **Can you think outside the box (or board)?** Some of the best business profile boards are ones that aren't obvious topics but are great fun (and a cool tie-in to the organization), such as the *Today* show's peacock board or Lindt Chocolate's Fashionable Chocolate board (as seen in Figure 4-3).

Figure 4-1:
Betty
Crocker's
Whoopie
Pies board.

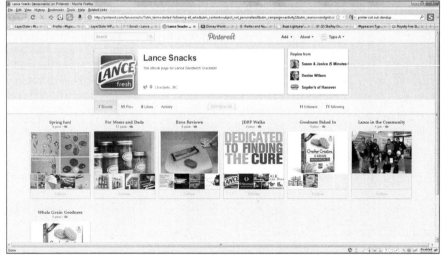

Figure 4-2:
A profile with boards that don't have many pins.

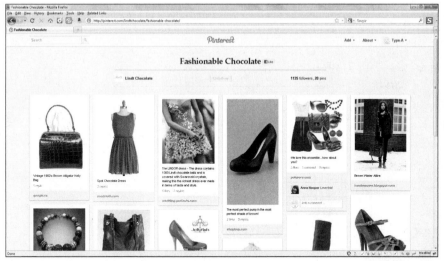

Figure 4-3:
Lindt Chocolate has a Fashionable Chocolate board featuring couture with a cocoa spin.

✔ **Are you thinking of search engines or human emotions?** Pinterest as a community loves to be impressed by creativity, but if you create a board with a straightforward name, it performs better in Google searches. If you create a board name that is fun and creative, however, it engages better on Pinterest. I recommend a mix of boards that say clearly what they are (like simple and clear titles such as "Dinner Recipes" and "Mason Jar Crafts") with those that show off your imagination (for example, I have "To Stuff in Your Suitcase" and "Smartphone Bling" for my business profile).

✔ **Is this a self-promotional board?** Although most of your boards should be created because the topic is interesting and related to (but not about) your brand, it is okay and oftentimes expected for you to create boards that are self-promotional. Look for ways to make it more engaging than "Stuff I Sell." For example, Sony Electronics doesn't simply have a "Sony Products" board. They have one dedicated to retro products just for fun, as well as a Brand New Sony Products board (see Figure 4-4) and a Sony on Sale board. Both are clearly promotional, but the slight spin in the board names makes them more interesting to potential customers.

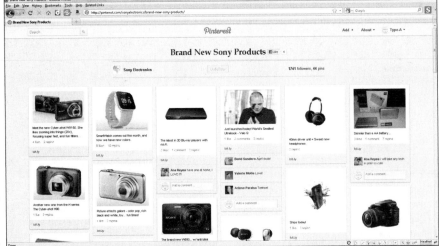

Figure 4-4:
Sony
Electronics'
Brand
New Sony
Products
board.

Naming your board

As you name a board, you want to find a name that is eye-catching as well as pretty clear about the topic of the board. As discussed earlier in this chapter, you can decide on a board by board basis whether you want to be search engine-friendly and just use a straightforward title or be funky and creative.

You can always go back and change a board title later. Keep in mind, however, that after you name a board, it sets the URL for the board. If you later change it, the URL will also change (and any links to the board directly will no longer work). Check out the "Editing your boards" section, later in this chapter, to find out how to rename your board.

You can have the same board name as other users because the final URL for your board will include your username (in a format of pinterest.com/ *USERNAME/ BOARDNAME*).

Board names have a 180-character limit, so you have to keep it brief. Also, the board name can get cut short in some instances, such as on your profile page. Avoid using any more than seven words.

Choosing a category

Pinterest allows people to browse by category, so be sure to choose a category that accurately describes your board.

For your brand or business, you may find a few topics are used by several boards and that is okay. In most instances, identifying a category for your board is pretty clear. Pinterest has several categories that cover a wide variety of topics. Click the down-pointing arrow on the right end of the Board Category field and use the drop-down menu (refer to Figure 4-5) to choose the one that best fits. Again, you can change this later. (See the "Editing your boards" section later in this chapter, to find out how.)

Figure 4-5:
The
category
drop-down
menu.

You're limited to the category options Pinterest makes available. Sometimes boards don't fit well in any category, and sometimes they would fit perfectly in two or more categories. I wouldn't agonize over this: Pick one that is the best fit and know that it is simple to move it to another category later.

Creating a new board

To create a new board on Pinterest, follow these steps:

1. **Sign in to your Pinterest account and click the Add+ button in the top-right corner of the Pinterest home page.**

   The Add dialog box appears and presents you with three choices: Add a Pin, Upload a Pin, and Create a Board. (See Figure 4-6.)

Figure 4-6:
The Add
dialog box
lets you add
pins or
create a
new board.

2. **Click the Create a Board option.**

   The Create a Board dialog box appears.

3. **Enter the basic information about your board: the name, category, and who can pin on this board (see Figure 4-7).**

   Check out the following sections for more information on naming, categorizing, and deciding who can contribute to your board. For more on group boards, see the next section.

4. **Click the Create Board button.**

As you're creating a board, it doesn't have a spot for a description. After you create your board, click the Edit Board button in the top-middle of your board and add a description. This isn't necessary, but it does appear at the top of the page when someone visits your board. You can also find out more about editing your board later in this chapter.

Creating collaborative group boards

One of the best and most fun tools for a business or organization on Pinterest is the collaborative group board option. A group board is one that allows other Pinterest users to contribute, or pin, to it.

Figure 4-7:
Choose a
board name,
category,
and
contributors
for your
new board.

Create a Board		
Board Name		
Board Category	Select a Category	▼
Who can pin?	✱ 👤 Just Me ○ 👥👥 Me + Contributors	
Create Board		

Although there are some really annoying ways to run a group board (such as self-promoting too heavily on a group board) and there are ineffective ways (adding people who never actually pin to a group board due to lack of interest), when it works well, it is Pinterest at possibly its most engaging for a business.

You can use your web site, blog, social networks, or e-mail newsletter to invite people to apply to be a board collaborator. This is a great way to find people who are passionate about your business or the topics you cover in your Pinterest profile. A free and easy tool to collect names is to use Google Docs. I used it to find attendees of my conference who were interested in collaborating (as you can see with the Google Doc form in Figure 4-8).

You can only add someone to a group board if they follow your profile (not just select boards) and you follow that member's profile.

Figure 4-8: Using a Google Doc form to collect applications for group board members.

Although quite a few options for collecting applications exist — such as other paid form services like Formsite.com or online survey software like SurveyMonkey.com — I recommend Google Docs for its simplicity, ease of exporting and sharing, and the free price tag.

In fact, I created a sample Pinterest group board signup form that you can feel free to access, copy, and modify as you wish. You can find it at `http://bit.ly/pinterestform`. Click File, and then Make a Copy to save it to your own Docs so you can edit the form and share it. Alternately, you can create a form in Google Docs from scratch with the following instructions.

To create a Pinterest group board interest form in Google Docs, follow these steps:

1. **Go to** `http://docs.google.com`.

   If you don't already have a free Google account, you need to sign up for one first.

2. **At the top left, click the Create button and then select Form.**

   This takes you to a page where you can begin to create and edit your form (as shown in Figure 4-9).

3. **Give your form a name and a description in the first two fields, as seen in Figure 4-10.**

   You cannot add someone to a board unless you follow their profile and they follow yours. It can be helpful in the introductory text here to remind anyone filling out the form to follow your Pinterest profile if they want to be added to one of your boards and include a link to the profile.

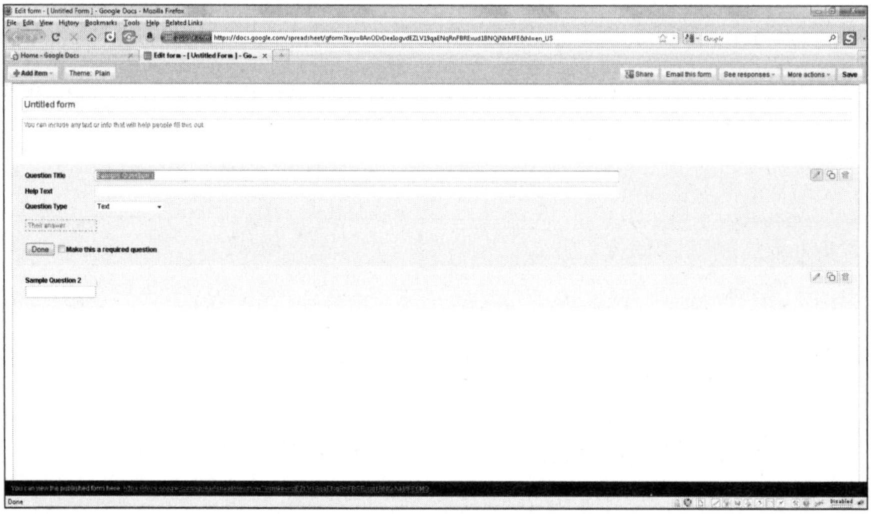

Figure 4-9:
A blank
Google
form.

4. **Directly below that, your first question is ready for your editing (see Figure 4-11).**

5. **Enter your first question where it says Question Title.**

   Here you can change the form question to ask what you would like, select the type of question (as seen in the drop-down menu in Figure 4-12), determine whether the question is required and so on.

Figure 4-10: Fill out the name and description of your form.

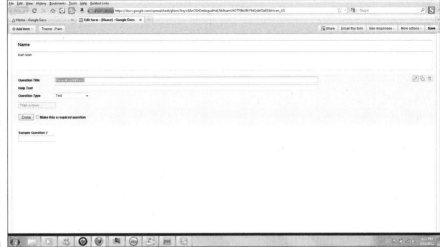

Figure 4-11: Mouse over the sample question to display icons to edit it.

Figure 4-12:
Selecting
the type of
question in
a Google
Docs form.

Here are some basic questions to include in your form:

- The URL to a person's Pinterest profile (so you can follow them and add them to your board)

- Name and e-mail address in case you need to get in touch (you can use the Help text on that question to let people know their e-mail address will not be publicized, sold, or shared)

- Twitter URL

- A check box question asking which boards they wish to collaborate on (if you will have multiple group boards).

6. **Click the Done button for the first question.**

   You should see a second question ready to edit below it. Create more form questions by mousing over the question you just did and clicking the duplicate icon. Repeat until you have the questions you need.

7. **Click Save (in the upper right corner).**

   The link to the live form is at the bottom of the page. Click it to look over your form before you share. On the Edit Form page, you will also see a number of other options, including changing the theme (at the top left). Under See Responses, you can view a summary or a spreadsheet that can be exported to Excel, and under More Actions, you can get code to embed the form onto your website and edit the confirmation people receive when they complete the form.

After you save, you see the form on your main `http://docs.google.com` page. Clicking the name of the form allows you to set notifications when someone submits the form, view the spreadsheet of results, edit the form, and share it with other members of your team.

There are many fun ways to use a group board to engage, to collaborate between staff members, and even to get feedback from customers. They include

- ✔ **Collaborating on work projects.** Share articles that offer tips on a specific industry or case studies that are relevant to the staff.

- ✔ **Sharing inspiration and ideas.** A home décor shop, for example, could include collaborators on boards related to specific colors or rooms. A tech company could have a group board featuring cutting edge gadgets.

- ✔ **Letting your customers, readers, or clients self-promote.** You can include a board that features projects they created using your products, or posts about your business. Better yet, simply have a board where they can share their own stuff and that allows you to promote them.

- ✔ **Promoting a joint cause or topic.** Share content that is relevant such as statistics on the issue, ways to donate or volunteer, and stories of people helped by the cause.

- ✔ **Share seasonal or topical content.** Create a holiday cookie board to collect and share recipes or a Mother's Day board to share crafts for kids to make gifts.

To create a group board, select Me + Contributors as you create the board. If you want to make an existing board into a group board, follow these instructions (skipping to Step 2 if you already have a group board and want instructions to add members):

1. **On your Pinterest profile page, find the board you want to make a group board and click the Edit Board button.**

   This takes you to the board edit page.

2. **Scroll down and select the Me + Contributors option (see Figure 4-13).**

3. **Type the beginning of the first name of the member you wish to add, or paste the e-mail address of the person you wish to invite and click Add to add that member to the group board.**

   You can add members by their actual first and last name as listed in their Pinterest profile (not user name) or you can invite by e-mail address. Figure 4-14 shows what happens if you start typing a member name in the text box: Pinterest automatically populates a list of possible matches, and you can select the right person from the list. Then just click the Add button next to the name. To invite someone via e-mail, type or paste in e-mail addresses one at a time in the field that appears when you click Me + Contributors and then click Add.

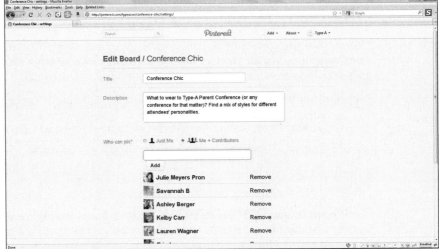

Figure 4-13:
Choosing
the group
board
option.

Figure 4-14:
You can add
contributors
to a board.

If you have more than one staff member or firm employee handling your business Pinterest account, or you are juggling both a business and personal account, consider adding those profiles as members of the business account's group boards. For the person juggling a personal and business account, it makes it so much easier to keep boards populated with content. For multiple people managing a business account, it makes it easier for each person to regularly contribute, even at times when they are not logged into the account.

Rearranging Your Boards

After you create some boards, you may want to rearrange them to bring your favorite, most popular, or most well-pinned boards to the top. To rearrange your boards, follow these instructions:

1. **Go to your profile page by clicking your name in the top-right corner of the screen.**

   Towards the top center of your profile screen, mouse over the screen icon with left and right arrows just to the right of the Edit Profile button (see Figure 4-15) and you will see the words Rearrange Boards.

2. **Click the Rearrange Boards screen icon.**

   This puts your profile into board rearranging mode. Where the icon was before you now see a red box with a checkmark.

3. **Click and hold on a board to move it, and then release the mouse button when you have the board where you want it.**

   Figure 4-16 shows how to drag and drop a board to a new position.

   Move as many boards as you like.

4. **Click the red checkmark button.**

   This saves your arrangement.

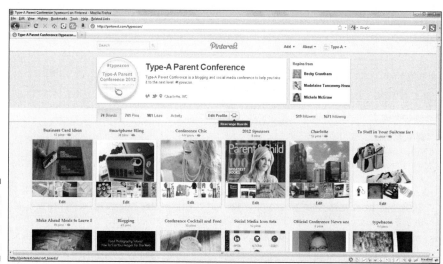

Figure 4-15: Clicking the Rearrange Boards icon.

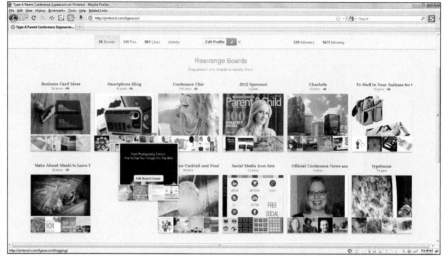

Figure 4-16:
Rearrange
your boards
by dragging
and
dropping.

Editing Your Board Cover Photo

A new feature of Pinterest is the ability to change the default, larger thumbnail image shown in your profile for each board. The cover photo is the
largest photo at the top of your board on your profile, just above four small
thumbnails (as seen in Figure 4-17).

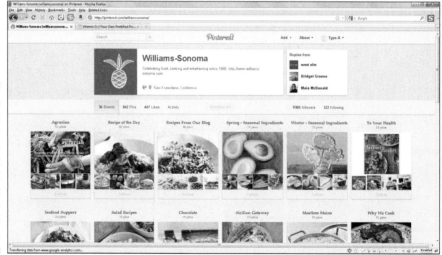

Figure 4-17:
Each board
has a cover
photo, the
largest
thumbnail
shown on
your pro-
file's board
page.

To edit your board cover photo, use these steps:

1. **From the home page, click your name in the right corner.**

   This takes you to your profile page, which defaults to a view of your boards.

2. **Mouse over the board you want to edit.**

   The Edit Board Cover button appears (see Figure 4-18).

Figure 4-18:
Revealing
the Edit
Board Cover
button.

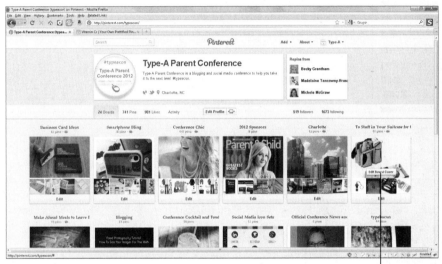

The Edit Board Cover button appears

3. **Click the button.**

   A dialog box appears and allows you to select your board cover pin.

4. **Scroll the right and left arrow buttons to see all images pinned on that board (see Figure 4-19).**

   Navigate until you find the image you want to use as your board cover. When you find the one you want, you can move it around to center it as you wish.

5. **Click the Set Cover button.**

   This returns you to your profile page, and you see the image you selected as the board's cover photo.

The image appears on your profile page just as it does at Step 4 in the previous list. This means that images sometimes have key elements cropped off the photo entirely even if you move and adjust it. In some cases, that may not be desirable, so be sure to review each thumbnail carefully in that preview panel before selecting one to set as your board cover photo.

Figure 4-19:
Selecting
your cover
image.

You can repeat this process for all of your boards, or you can opt to leave all of your boards at the default settings. The default setting shows the latest pinned image as the large photo on your profile list of boards.

You don't have to be limited to the obvious when it comes to board appearances on your profile. There is a fun tool that allows you to customize your board so that all of the images form one puzzle-like image (see Figure 4-20). You can find the tool at `http://vitamincr.com/pinterest/creative-boards/your-own-prettified-pinterest-board-in-30s-with-this-hacksplice-tool/`.

Figure 4-20:
A tool for
creating a
collage and
puzzle-style
look for
your board
images.

Editing Your Boards

At some point, you might want to edit one or more of your boards for various reasons (such as renaming it, adding a description, or categorizing the board).

Be aware that changing the name of a board also changes its web URL. If you or anyone else has linked to your board using the old link, they get an error message. For example, `pinterest.com/`*`yourname`*`/`*`yourboard`* becomes `pinterest.com/`*`yourname`*`/`*`newboardname`*. Any links to the board from outside Pinterest should be updated with the new URL. If someone besides you has linked to it, there's likely little you can do to correct that (except approach each person who linked and ask them to update their links), so those links will be dead.

To edit a board, follow these steps:

1. **Visit your profile by clicking your name in the top-right corner of the screen.**

2. **On your profile page, find the board that's in need of some editing attention and click the Edit button for that board.**

   The Edit Board screen appears, as shown in Figure 4-21.

3. **Change the title, description, who can pin on the board, and/or the category.**

4. **When you're done making changes, click the Save Settings button.**

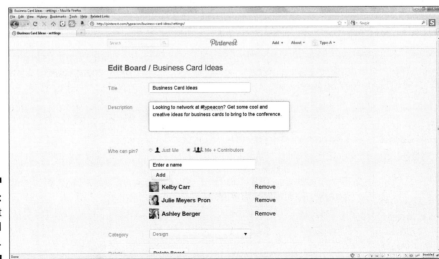

Figure 4-21: The Edit Board screen.

Deleting a Board

In most instances, you edit a board if there's something about it you don't like. Still, sometimes boards don't make sense anymore. The boards you created when Pinterest prompted you at login might turn out to make no sense for you, for example.

 If you want to delete a board because another one is too similar, you might consider first repinning the pins from the board about to be deleted onto the one that will remain. Otherwise, all your pins on the board about to be deleted will go poof.

If you need to delete a board, follow these steps:

1. **On your profile, find the board you want to delete.**

2. **Click the Edit button on the board.**

   The Edit Board page appears. (Refer to Figure 4-21.)

3. **Click the Delete Board button and confirm.**

Leaving a Collaborative Board

You may find that people add you to collaborative boards that you don't want to participate in (in the past, members did not have to request permission to add you, for example, or you might have agreed at one time and change your mind later when you see inappropriate content). This can be an especially sensitive issue for a Pinterest account you create for the purpose of marketing. You may not want to be added to a board that is heavy with salty humor if you own a family-oriented business, for example. Deleting yourself as a contributor from a collaborative board isn't terribly intuitive, but it is simple. You can remove yourself from a group board by following these instructions:

1. **Navigate to your profile and find the group board you want to leave.**

2. **Click the Edit button.**

   The Edit Board page appears. (Refer to Figure 4-21.)

3. **Scroll down until you find your name on the list of pinners for that board, as shown in Figure 4-22.**

Figure 4-22:
You can remove your profile from a group board.

4. **Click Remove to the right of your name.**

   You're removed from the board and can no longer pin items to it. It will also no longer appear on your profile.

If you created the board, you cannot remove yourself from it. You see only the option to remove members you added or delete the board.

Chapter 5

Pinning and Repinning

In This Chapter

▶ Finding great images to pin

▶ Repinning

▶ Using hashtags, mentions, and price tags

*A*fter you have created boards, you need to pin and repin images to them so they don't look barren. Populating new boards with original pins by hunting down excellence on the web can be incredibly time-consuming, but fortunately you can also repin to fill your boards with imagery.

It can be tempting to create only pins that directly promote your business, brand, or organization. In fact, you may notice many big brands on Pinterest do just that. Resist the urge! It not only is a huge turn-off to other members, but people are in fact less likely to repin your stuff (or even follow you) if all you do is talk (or pin) about yourself. Self-promotional pins should be by far the minority of your pins. (I recommend no more than 20 percent.) You should also avoid doing a bunch of self-promotional pins right in a row. Stagger them.

Adding a Pin with a Website URL

When you find a web page that you know you'll want to return to, as long as the page has an image for pinning, you can follow a few simple steps to pin it by using the web page's URL.

Unless you have a reason, don't pin from the home page for a site to share articles and blog posts. An image from a post will move off the home page, and later on, people won't be able to find the source. If you see a post on a blog home page, click the title to go to the *permalink* (the longer, deep link that takes a reader directly to a post instead of the list of posts on the home page) for that post and use that URL.

When you find an image you want to pin, follow these instructions to pin it to your board:

1. **Copy the URL of the page where the image appears.**

   You do this by going to the page where the image is located. In your browser's address bar, click and highlight the entire URL. Then copy that address.

2. **Use your web browser to navigate to** `http://pinterest.com` **and log in.**

3. **Click the Add + button at the top-right corner of the screen.**

   The Add dialog box appears.

4. **Click the Add a Pin button.**

   The Add a Pin dialog box appears, as shown in Figure 5-1.

5. **Paste the URL you copied in Step 1 into the URL field in the Add a Pin dialog box.**

6. **Click the Find Images button.**

   The Add a Pin dialog box expands to show these additional options (see Figure 5-2):

   • Images from the page

   • A drop-down list of your boards

   • A description text box

Figure 5-1:
Paste the
URL into the
Add a Pin
dialog box.

Figure 5-2:
Add a pin
with a URL.

7. **To choose an image from the page, click the Next or Prev arrow (refer to Figure 5-2) until you find the image you want to pin.**

   You can select only one image at a time from the page.

8. **Use the drop-down list of your boards to select the board for the pin.**

   If none of your boards suit this new pin, you can create a new board on the fly by scrolling to the bottom of your board list, entering a board name where it says Create New Board, and clicking Create.

9. **Type a description of the pin in the Describe Your Pin text box.**

   Don't forget that viewers of your pin will have no context for the image. They won't see the title of the source web page that it came from. Be sure to not only use the description to say how you feel about what you're pinning (such as "great tips") but to clearly say exactly what it is (such as "great tips on cleaning the kitchen"). You can also have fun with the description to make it more engaging, to add your personality stamp to it, and to give your followers a sense of why you pinned it.

10. **Click the Pin It button.**

    You're taken directly to your pin's page.

If you add a pin from a website, you don't need to provide a source in the description. Pinterest automatically links the image and the pin to the original URL you provided, and it shows the main domain name of the website on the pin's page.

Installing the Pinterest Pin It Button

To make it easier to pin great images as you browse the Internet, install the Pin It button to your web browser toolbar. When it's installed, you can click the Pin It button from any web page and the app will look for images to pin from that page. To install the Pin It button, follow these steps:

1. **Log in to your Pinterest account and mouse over the About button in the top-right corner of the Pinterest home page.**

   A drop-down menu appears.

2. **Choose Pin It Button from the menu.**

   The Pinterest Goodies page appears.

3. **Scroll to the top of the Goodies page to find the Pin It button, as shown in Figure 5-3.**

   Pinterest can tell which browser you're using and provides browser-specific instructions for installing the Pin It button.

4. **Follow the instructions on Pinterest for installing the Pin It button in your particular browser.**

   The steps can vary slightly from browser to browser. Most instructions involve dragging the Pin It button image onto the bookmark toolbar at the top of your browser window.

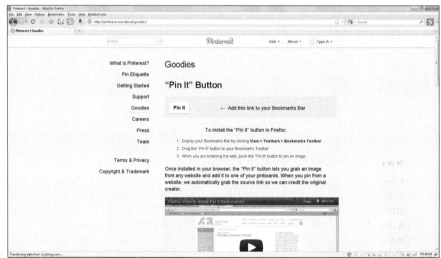

Figure 5-3:
The Pin It
button and
instructions.

Pinterest provides a video on how to install the Pin It button. If you don't see the video right away, scroll down a little bit on the page.

Using the Pin It Button to Add a Pin

The Pin It button makes it quick and easy to pin images during your normal web browsing. Instead of copying and pasting URLs and going between Pinterest and the site you're browsing, you can do it all in a couple of clicks. You don't even need to leave the site you're browsing.

1. **Navigate to the page with the image you'd like to pin to a board.**

   You should already be logged in to Pinterest.

2. **Click the Pinterest Pin It button on your bookmark toolbar, shown in Figure 5-4.**

   A new page appears showing any pinnable images from the page. Below each image are the dimensions of the image in pixels.

   Keep in mind that larger images look better on Pinterest than smaller ones. Also be aware that some images simply can't be pinned due to the coding, and also because Pinterest allows sites to opt out of being pinned. If either is the case, you can't pin those images.

The Pin It toolbar button

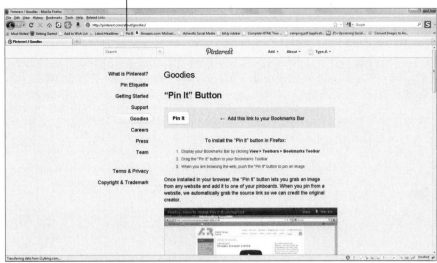

Figure 5-4:
The Pin It button on the bookmark toolbar.

3. **Click the image you want to pin.**

   The Create Pin pop-up window appears.

4. **Use the drop-down list to select the board you want to pin to, and then type a description in the box provided.**

   What if you don't yet have a board that this new pin belongs on? You can create a new board by following the instructions in Step 8.

5. **Click the Pin It button.**

   You then see a dialog box that gives you the option to view your pin, (if you have Twitter integrated) tweet your pin, or (if you have Facebook integrated) share your pin on Facebook. If you choose none of the options, eventually the site returns you to the page you were beforehand.

Uploading an Image as a Pin

You can also upload your own image as a pin instead of having to pin content that already exists online. For marketing purposes, this can be a great option for revealing behind-the-scenes imagery, showing off new products before they hit shelves, or giving a human face to your business by sharing photos of your CEO or staff.

This method is handy but also potentially can be a copyright violation. Unlike a pin from a website, a direct image upload doesn't link to its original source.

Image upload can be great for pinning interesting sights you see during your day or in your travels, for example.

You should upload only images that you take yourself, and you should make that clear in the way you word the pin description. For example, the description could be something like, "We're in Paris! Here's a picture I took of the Eiffel Tower." Uploading other people's images can be a copyright violation. The person who takes a picture typically owns the rights to the image. By explaining that you took the photo, you make it clear who owns the image and that you didn't violate anyone's copyrights.

Be careful to avoid taking photos of copyrighted material, such as an entire article or spread in a magazine or anything that completely reproduces someone else's copyrighted image.

To upload an image as a pin, follow these steps:

1. **Use your browser to navigate to** `http://pinterest.com` **and log in.**

2. **Click the Add + button in the top-right corner of the screen.**

   The Add dialog box appears.

3. **Click the Upload a Pin button.**

   The Upload a Pin dialog box appears.

4. **Click the Browse button to find the image on your computer's hard drive.**

   The File Upload dialog box appears, as shown in Figure 5-5.

5. **Select the image to upload and click Open.**

6. **The Upload a Pin dialog box expands to show the image as well as a drop-down list and a description text box.**

7. **Use the drop-down list to select a board.**

8. **Type a description of your pin in the text box.**

9. **Click the Pin It button.**

   You're taken directly to the pin's page. Although you can upload images, you can't directly upload video.

Although uploaded images do not include a link connected to the pin, there is a workaround. After you upload a pin image, visit the pin page and click the Edit button at the top. You will be taken to a page to change details about the pin (see Figure 5-6), which includes a spot to enter a link (a website URL). Include a related URL here, such as your own web page if it's a self-promotional image you have uploaded.

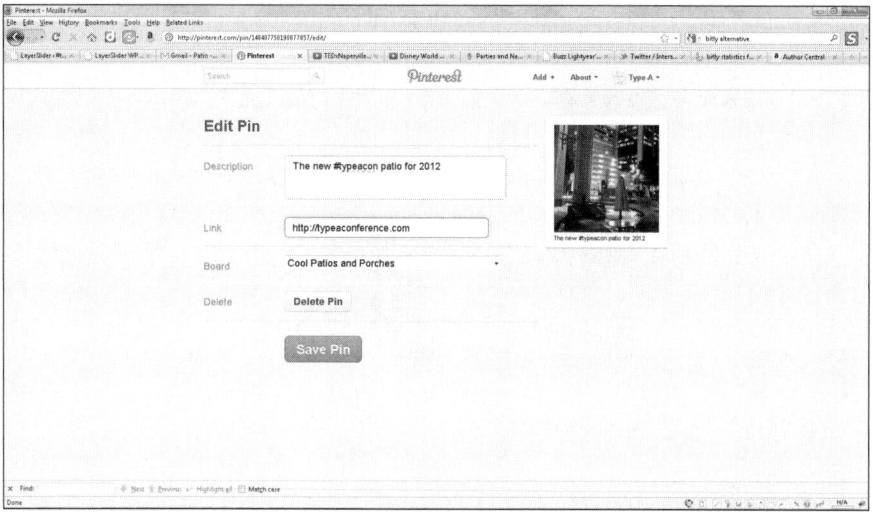

Figure 5-6:
Editing a
pin to add a
link.

Repinning

When you share another user's existing pin, placing that user's pin on one of your own boards, that's called *repinning*. Repinning makes it easy to create some great pins and to do it consistently without consuming a lot of time. A browse of your stream of people you follow can often produce several images that are great to repin in seconds, even.

Beyond that, repinning is a great way to support and engage with the Pinterest community. It shows that you are being social and not simply a brand up on a pedestal expecting customers to rave without any sort of reciprocation.

To repin a pin, follow these steps:

1. **Find a pin that you would like to repin and mouse over it.**

   Three buttons appear: Repin, Like, and Comment. (See Figure 5-7.)

2. **Click the Repin button.**

   The Repin dialog box appears.

3. **Use the drop-down list to choose which of your boards to use for the repin.**

   If needed, you can also use this drop-down list to create a new board.

4. **Type a description of the pin in the text box.**

   Often you can use the existing description, but sometimes you might need to change the description to your own words.

The Repin, Like, and Comment buttons

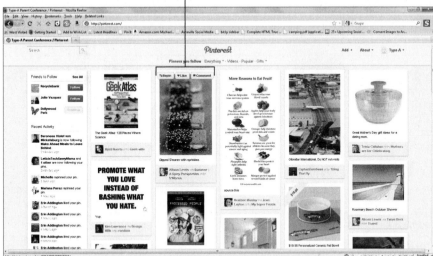

5. **Click the Pin It button.**

   A box flashes with the option to view the pin now. If you don't click it, you're taken back to the page where you repinned.

Finding pins to repin

You can find pins to repin in several ways. Your repins can come both from those Pinterest members you follow and from the general Pinterest membership.

Here are a few different methods for finding great pins to repin:

- **Browse the stream of people you follow.** You can do this by visiting the Pinterest homepage while logged in. It defaults to Pinners You Follow, which is also in the top menu.

- **Browse categories.** To browse the latest pins in a category, make sure you're logged in and from in the top menu mouse over (but don't click!) the Everything link in the top-middle of the screen. Click a category from the options.

- **Browse videos.** Much of the emphasis on Pinterest is on pictures and graphics, but you can also pin (and, thus, repin) videos. You can find videos to repin by clicking the Videos link in the top-middle of the screen, and then you can mouse over a video to access the Repin button.

✔ **Use the Pinterest Search feature.** Pinterest has a Search feature for finding pins, boards, and users. The Search text box is located in the top-left corner of any page on the site. You can type a search term in the Search text box and then click the Search button (the magnifying glass icon) to perform a search. After you've clicked the Search button, you see results. The default results are pins that match your terms. You can then filter your search results by boards or people by clicking your choice (a text link for Boards or People) just above the results.

✔ **Browse Everything.** Use the top menu to click Everything. This is a diverse mix of image types and topics, but can be a great way to discover pins to repin.

✔ **Browse Popular pins.** Use the top menu from the homepage and click Popular. This shows pins that have been repinned, liked, and commented on by many members. The great thing about browsing popular pins is these have already been vetted and proven to spark engagement.

Just because a pin is popular, however, doesn't mean it is a reflection on the quality of the pin or your likelihood to be repinned if you share it. A pin from a user with many followers could be popular only because of that member's popularity. Some popular pins also could be so prominent in everyone's Pinterest stream by that time that people are sick of seeing them. It's a good resource, but don't rely too heavily on sharing popular pins as a shortcut to success and engagement.

✔ **Browse Gifts.** From the homepage, make sure you're logged in and mouse over Gifts in the top menu. You can then browse pins by price range. These pins typically show products that have a price mentioned in the description. See more on adding a price tag to your pin later in this chapter.

✔ **Locate a specific user's pins.** To find a specific user's pins, conduct a search for the user's name or username and then click the People link below the Search text box. The search results page changes to show profiles with the search term instead of pins.

✔ **Find pins from a specific website.** Although this trick isn't obvious, you can search for existing pins that have come from a specific website as well. The easiest way to do this is to enter the website's main domain in your browser's address bar in the format `pinterest.com/source/DOMAIN.COM`, replacing `DOMAIN.COM` with the site you're interested in.

Sharing a pin or repin on Facebook and Twitter

To share a pin on Twitter or Facebook as you pin, you must have the social network integrated into your Pinterest account (as described in Chapter 2).

If you don't have it integrated, you can instead share directly from a pin page (sharing buttons are situated to the right of the pin image on its page). After they're integrated, it's easy to share a repin or a pin on those sites.

As you pin or repin, you'll see the option to check the boxes for Twitter and Facebook. (See Figure 5-8.) When you do, that pin will be posted (on Twitter as a tweet with a link to the pin; on Facebook as an update with a thumbnail of the image and a link to the pin). You can also integrate Pinterest into your Facebook timeline, which will be covered in Chapter 8. Integrating them displays a section on your Timeline showing all of your Pinterest activity.

You can also share your pins in the same manner — by selecting the check box for Facebook and/or Twitter — when the pin description box pops up.

You can get some benefits out of tweeting and Facebook sharing your pins. Sharing helps spread the word that you're on Pinterest and attract followers from your other social networks. It also encourages people on those networks to repin your pins.

It can be easy to pin or repin several things in a very short period of time. You might want to limit which pins you share on Facebook and Twitter so you don't annoy your followers on those networks.

Figure 5-8:
You can
share on
Twitter and
Facebook as
you repin.

Using Hashtags, Mentions, and Price Tags

You can use some tricks to enhance your pins or add to their functionality. You can use hashtags similar to those found on Twitter, you can tag members' names in pin descriptions, and you can add a price tag ribbon that will appear in the top-left corner of a pin.

Using hashtags

A *hashtag* is a way of tagging a term so that the term becomes *clickable* (this means that when you see a hashtag, you can click on it). You do this by adding a # at the beginning of a word, such as #pinterest.

If you are used to using hashtags on Twitter, be aware they function differently on Pinterest. Clicking a Pinterest hashtag doesn't give you results that also have that hashtag. What it does is conduct a search for that word after the # symbol.

To view results for the search term when you see it in a pin description, click any word that starts with a #. (See Figure 5-9.) Clicking the hashtag takes you to the search results for that word.

Figure 5-9:
Click a hashtag in a pin description to see pins that match that search term.

A hash tag in a pin description

TIP

If you use a hashtag, it should be something that people would want to search for or be a popular word or term. If you only want pins specific to your campaign or project, use something so distinctive it is unlikely the search will turn up anything except pins related to your project.

Tagging member names in pins

In a pin description, you can tag another Pinterest member to draw their attention to the pin. You must both be following one another (both following all via profile, not simply following certain boards). Tagging them also makes their profile name in the pin description link to that person's profile.

To tag a member while pinning, repinning, or commenting, follow these steps:

1. **In a pin description or a comment, type the @ character and the first letter(s) of the name of the person you want to tag in the description without a space.**

   Type **@a**, for example, to tag someone whose name starts with A.

   A drop-down list of friends whose names start with that letter appears, as shown in Figure 5-10.

2. **From the drop-down list, select the name of the person you want to tag.**

   The name is filled out in that spot in the description.

Figure 5-10: Pinterest creates a list of friends based on the letters you type.

3. **Finish writing your comment or description and then click the Comment or Repin button to publish.**

   After you tag the person, the description of the pin features her name, and it will be linked to her profile page.

Including a price tag in a pin

Including a price tag with a pin is amazingly simple and the results are eye-catching. When writing a description of a pin, include a dollar sign followed by the number of the price, such as either $1 or $3.25. This feature is ideal when pinning a product. When a price tag has been added to a pin, the pin is displayed with a price tag ribbon in its top-left corner. (See Figure 5-11.)

Anytime you include a dollar sign in a pin, it adds a price tag ribbon to the image. Some pins simply refer to a price to do a project, where a price tag in a traditional sense might not make sense. If you wish to avoid having a price tag on a pin, don't use the $ symbol (for example, type **five dollars** instead of **$5**). You should also be aware that Pinterest is very literal and formatting is particular. For example, if you type $1 million, it will display $1. Instead, you need to type $1,000,000 into your description. You can use commas.

Price tags

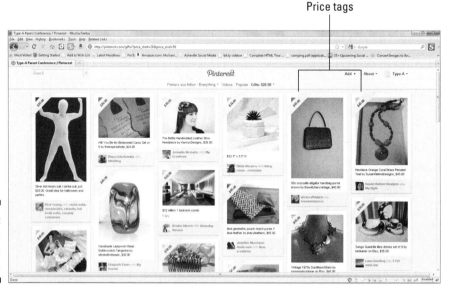

Figure 5-11:
A pin with a price tag ribbon.

When you use the price tag feature on a pin, the pin is pulled into the Gifts section, which you can find from the Pinterest home page. Click the Gifts link in the top-middle area of the Pinterest home page. Under the Gifts menu, pins are organized by price.

Chapter 6

Getting Active on Pinterest

In This Chapter

▶ Finding time to pin

▶ Interacting with comments and likes

▶ Going mobile with Pinterest

S o you've joined Pinterest. Rock on! You're all set, right? Sorry, nope. Getting an account set up and creating some boards and pins is just the beginning. To thrive on Pinterest, you need to consistently be active on the social network.

In this chapter, I talk about how to find time to work Pinterest into your busy life, how to interact with your followers, and the benefits of going mobile with Pinterest.

Finding Time for Pinterest

Before you groan, know that I understand you are busy. I understand you might already be juggling Twitter, Facebook, Google+ and a number of other social networks. I understand that you might really prefer to put your energy into the business you are promoting, instead of promoting the business.

I feel the same way. I use a few tactics to make Pinterest more manageable while remaining very active on the site.

Here are a few tips I have discovered to be extremely active and engaged on Pinterest without giving up sleep hours to find the time:

✔ **Go mobile.** If you have any smartphone with a touch screen or a tablet, you can use Pinterest mobile or a Pinterest app anytime. Pinterest Mobile can be found at `m.pinterest.com`, and there is an official Pinterest iPhone app by Cold Brew Labs (just search the App Store). Increasingly, other mobile apps are being released, such as SpinPicks, for both iPhone and Android. Search your mobile platform's app store or marketplace for Pinterest. It can be great to sneak in a few repins, comments, and likes while drinking your morning coffee, standing in line at the bank, waiting to pick up the kids at soccer practice, lying in bed before going to sleep, and so on.

✔ **Pin throughout the day.** You should have a schedule of daily time dedicated to Pinterest if you plan to use it earnestly as a marketing tool, but it also helps to view it as an integral part of what you do online while surfing the web (be sure you have the pin it button discussed in the last chapter) or while you're out and about using your camera phone.

✔ **Put a time limit on Pinterest sessions.** If you find Pinterest is a little too mesmerizing, set a time limit on each session so you don't get carried away. Fifteen minutes on Pinterest, for example, can result in dozens of repins. It truly doesn't take much time.

Setting a Pinterest Schedule

To get active on Pinterest, you need to not only dedicate time to the site but also consistently use it daily if possible. Your schedule will depend heavily on who is managing the account and how many hours per week can be devoted to Pinterest.

Here are some tasks I would consider bare essentials, and a minimum amount of time to devote to them to maintain an active account:

✔ **Repinning:** At least 15 minutes daily and preferably broken into three or four sessions.

✔ **Pinning new content:** At least 15 minutes weekly.

✔ **Board creation and maintenance:** Such as categorizing or adding cover photos, 15 minutes weekly.

✔ **Commenting and liking pins:** 15 minutes weekly.

✔ **Adding followers:** 15 minutes weekly.

Devoting more time is obviously ideal, but these are minimum guidelines to maintaining a decent Pinterest presence. Although it is okay to occasionally have a few days of inactivity during a crazy period, for the most part, you want to be active at least repinning on weekdays.

User activity on Pinterest peaks between 5 and 7 a.m. EST and again between 5 and 7 p.m. EST, according to SEOmoz (www.SEOmoz.com). To see if you get the biggest bang (and responsiveness), experiment with pinning and repinning during those time frames.

To set up a Pinterest schedule, follow these steps:

1. **Determine your activity level.**

   When you first join Pinterest, it is important to be more active. You can probably scale back slightly after you have a decent amount of boards and pins.

2. **Set daily times to use Pinterest at a minimum.**

   Try to integrate Pinterest into your day. That means you can use Pinterest as you do research on the web, for example. For this, you want to determine the minimum amount of time you wish to devote to all Pinterest tasks each day (or weekday).

3. **Set a reminder to get on Pinterest.**

   After you are an active user, you probably will be so hooked on Pinterest that you won't need this. But for marketing purposes, until it becomes a daily habit, make sure you don't forget. You can use tools like your phone or computer's calendar to set up a repeating daily event (or on weekdays).

   If multiple people will manage the account, be sure to stagger the times you're all pinning. For example, you don't want all four staff members to pin Monday morning and no one else to pin the rest of the week. Divvy up days among those who will share the Pinterest duties.

4. **Reassess after the first month to see if the schedule is working.**

   You want to be sure you have enough time set aside to do Pinterest properly, and you also might realize that a certain time of day is really bad for pinning. You could shift more time the day before, for example.

I actually use Pinterest on mobile far more frequently than I use Pinterest on my computer. There are a few reasons for that. I always have my phone, so I can sneak in some pins during down times. (I think I would be far less active if I used it only at my desk on my computer.) Pinterest's mobile site and the Pinterest iPhone app are simplified, more focused versions of Pinterest that I actually find easier to use than the web version.

Finding Shareable Content to Pin

The best way to win at pinning is to share amazing images. Great images make people laugh or cry, stand out in a page full of pins, evoke a memory or spark an interest, and generally grab attention.

Beyond that, people like pins that link to excellent content and resources.

A pin is much more than its image. Yes, that is the predominant feature of a pin, but a high quality pin also has a clear, catchy description and, ideally, links to wonderful content that goes beyond just the image itself (to a tutorial, a list, a how-to and so on).

Although anything with an image is technically pinnable, certain types of pins do that very well. By all means, do not limit yourself to this short list of types of pins (be creative, experiment), but here are some basic types of content that perform well as pins:

- **Food and recipe pins:** These are pins with images of a delicious-looking dish, and ideally a link to a high-quality recipe with a clear description and instructions. Figure 6-1 is a pin that was repinned more than 165 times. You can also find the detailed recipe and tutorial it links to at `http://sugarswings.blogspot.com/2011/08/rainbow-ice-cream-cone-cake-bites.html`.

- **Craft and DIY pins:** These are pins with beautiful, attractive, or cute projects that link to a detailed tutorial with step-by-step instructions.

- **Quotes:** Images of quotes are frequently repinned, especially if the quote is empowering, motivational, or moving. Many blog posts now have images with quotes (likely to encourage people to pin them, in fact). You can find an interesting tool, Share As Image, at `http://shareas image.com`, which allows you to copy text on an article to make it into a pinnable quote. You can use the free version, or pay $2.99 for a pro version with color and font options.

Figure 6-1:
Recipe and food tutorials are popular on Pinterest.

✔ **Fashion pins and outfits:** The site Polyvore (`http://polyvore.com`), where you can put together entire outfits and share the ensemble, is particularly popular on Pinterest.

✔ **Pop culture icons:** Pins with products, posters, and pretty much anything related to popular (especially geeky) icons like *Star Wars* (see Figure 6-2), *Harry Potter*, *Doctor Who*, and so on get repinned and get comments frequently.

✔ **Pretty décor and design:** It helps that a good design or décor pin is usually lovely to see passing in your Pinterest stream, but these pins get repinned a lot.

✔ **Wedding and event pins:** Wedding planning in particular is one of the more popular topics on Pinterest.

✔ **Cool or quirky products:** Not every product is going to get buzz on Pinterest, but ones that are unusual, stand out from other products, are new, or are aesthetically pretty do very well on Pinterest.

✔ **Jokes and humor:** This is not only a category on Pinterest, but extremely popular as a subject of pins.

✔ **Infographics:** It isn't much of a surprise considering the visual nature of Pinterest, but infographics (especially those related to social media) do very well on Pinterest. One thing to remember is that infographics have odd formatting for Pinterest (extremely long so that thumbnails are impossible to distinguish), so keep that in mind and limit them to the most interesting ones.

Figure 6-2:
Star Wars
images are
pinned and
repinned
often.

This list is by no means comprehensive, but it gives you a general idea of what you will see pinned a lot on Pinterest and what engages well there. Still, I believe every niche has a following to find on Pinterest and any type of pin can do well if it is interesting and compelling.

Commenting and Liking

Just pinning and repinning isn't enough to truly socialize on Pinterest. While it is easily the bulk of what many members do, you also want to be sure to interact with pins in other ways. Pinterest has very little "talking." It is very much a, "Show, don't tell," site.

There are no status updates, and you can't send messages to members privately (at least not of this writing). Beyond speaking to your audience there via pin descriptions, comments are the only other place to use words to interact. It might be easy to underestimate the value of commenting on Pinterest, but I wouldn't.

Some pins get a tremendous number of comments, and the result is a robust conversation. Here are a few reasons why commenting (at least from time to time) is a good idea:

- ✔ **It draws attention to your profile.** This is the case for the member whose pin you comment on, as well as anyone else who sees (or comments on) that pin. You can attract followers simply by being an active commenter.

- ✔ **It gives you a chance to further hone your brand's personality and human side.** If all you do is pin and repin, you are primarily broadcasting on Pinterest. If you comment, you are taking it a step further to conversing.

- ✔ **It helps people get to know you.** There is this interesting phenomenon online and on social networks that you may have noticed on other sites like Twitter and Facebook: When people start having conversations with you, they feel like they know you personally. When you are deciding who to hire or read or what product to buy, which do you choose? The big anonymous company or the friend who chit-chats with you on Pinterest?

Commenting doesn't need to dominate your time, and it shouldn't be forced. If you see a pin that sparks a thought in your mind, comment on it. Add a couple thoughts. It's that simple.

Don't use comments as a place to directly self-promote, or to talk about yourself or your company. Don't link to your own content unless you have a really compelling reason (for example, someone specifically asks a question that is answered by linking to it). That's because this behavior is viewed as anything from rudeness to spamming. Remember to be polite. It can be tempting to be snarky online when you are safely behind your computer screen, but it doesn't reflect on you or your organization well.

To comment on a pin from the home page or a search results page:

1. **From the results page, find the pin you want to comment on and mouse over the image.**

   Three buttons appear: Repin, Like, and Comment. See Figure 6-3.

The Repin, Like, and Comment buttons

Figure 6-3:
Finding the
Comment
button on
a pin.

2. **Click the Comment button.**

   Your cursor moves to the bottom of the pin in a box where you can type in your remarks.

3. **Type your comment and click the Comment button.**

   Your comment appears.

You reach a pin page when you click the pin image in search results or when you find a pin that is shared via its permalink on another site or social network. You might also be on a pin page to view its source or other statistics. To comment on a pin page:

1. **Scroll below the image pinned and find your profile picture with a box with Add a Comment inside (see Figure 6-4).**

   You may have to scroll more than once if a pin has several comments. This is the comment box.

Figure 6-4:
Commenting
on a pin
page.

2. **Click inside the box and type your comment.**

3. **Click the Post Comment button.**

   Your comment appears.

If you want to follow conversations on pins where you have commented, be sure to set up notifications. Do that by mousing over your name, clicking Settings, and clicking the E-mail Preferences button. There are several options, including one to receive an e-mail when someone else comments on a pin where you have commented.

Another way to interact with others is to like their pins. At first blush, liking and repinning might seem redundant, but there are times where it makes sense to use one or the other (or even both). A good comparison would be Facebook's Like versus Facebook's Share.

A like is an endorsement, a thumbs-up to what someone else shares on Pinterest. It only appears in your profile page after someone clicks the Likes filter. This is a text link that says a number followed by Likes at the top center of your profile page, right below your avatar and bio. A repin is interesting enough you want to push that image out to your own stream of followers, and it appears on their home page when you do, listing you as the pinner.

You might choose a like over a repin for a few reasons. Something might be interesting enough that you want to find it later for reference, but it might not be a good fit for your business or brand. You might even not have a board that is a good fit, and you might not foresee doing more pins on the same topic that would justify creating a board for this pin.

Whatever the reason, it is simple and fast to like a pin. On a results page, the home page or a pin page, mouse over the pin image. The Like button appears, and you should click it (see Figure 6-5). After you do, the button disappears. If you mouseover again, you can confirm it registered the Like if the button is now transparent.

Figure 6-5:
The Like button on a pin page.

Chapter 7

Getting Fans, Customers, and Clients to Follow You

In This Chapter

▶ Using multiple channels to attract followers

▶ Spreading the word at your store or location

▶ Joining Pinterest linkups to attract followers

I've talked a lot about engaging with other Pinterest users on Pinterest, but this chapter explains many other avenues for finding Pinterest followers. There are so many people from so many walks of life using Pinterest (millions, in fact), you could have current fans, customers, and clients who would love to follow you on Pinterest. They just need to know you are there first.

Although the logical place to seek out followers on a social network is other social networks, there are many other points of contact to find followers. Anywhere your message goes out — online, in print and in person, in fact — is another opportunity to get new Pinterest followers.

Don't push your Pinterest page until it is ready for public consumption (meaning your profile is complete, you have a profile picture, you have some followers and follow people back, you have a few boards, and all of your boards have a few pins at the minimum). First impressions go a long way, and someone who takes the time to check out your Pinterest page only to be disappointed may never return again. That said, it's okay for your account to look new, as long as it doesn't look incomplete.

Using Your Website, E-mail List, and Social Media Channels to Attract Followers

You probably already reach your audience or your customers in a variety of ways, and any (or all) of those methods can be used to spread the word about your Pinterest page. In many cases, just a few minutes to add a Pinterest icon, for example, can go a long way.

This doesn't require a massive dedication of time and resources (although if you have to pay to get all the changes done by a web developer, it could add up).

Promoting your Pinterest profile on your website or blog

First, look at your web presence, both a standard website and a blog if you have one. On either, you probably already have a place with social media icons to help people follow you (if you don't, you might want to consider adding them all!).

 If you use WordPress, you can find a number of plug-ins to add a Pinterest icon or widget. To find them, search the WordPress plug-ins directory for *Pinterest follow* or go to `http://wordpress.org/extend/plugins/search.php?q=pinterest+follow`.

Pinterest offers the code to create a Follow Me on Pinterest button on your site. To add it,

1. **While logged in, go to the home page, mouse over About in the top menu, and click Pin It Button.**

   This takes you to the Pinterest goodies page.

2. **Scroll down to Follow Button for Websites (see Figure 7-1).**

3. **Click the button or icon you would like to use on your website or blog.**

   Code that is customized for your profile is automatically generated to the right.

4. **Copy the code.**

   You need to paste it in the code on your own site (or a plain text widget in your blog's sidebar). If you don't know how to do this, have your web developer do it for you.

Figure 7-1:
Finding
the Follow
Button
code.

You can go with Pinterest's own code, or you can use a variation that is more suited to your website's colors, theme, or design. Simply Google "Pinterest icon" and you will find many results, including quite a few that are free. You can also hire a graphic designer to create one for you, such as the custom icon used in the top right of Figure 7-2.

Figure 7-2:
A custom
Pinterest
icon.

A custom Pinterest icon

If you use WordPress, there are also several widgets that will put a Follow Me on Pinterest button as well as thumbnails of your latest pins (as seen on the left of Figure 7-3).

Figure 7-3:
The Pinterest RSS Widget plug-in in the sidebar of my blog.

The Pinterest RSS Widget plug-in

Although the type of widget in Figure 7-3 takes up a decent amount of real estate on your site or blog, it is also attention-getting and gives people a preview of what to expect if they follow you on Pinterest. Even if you use a widget for a short period of time, it can help drive followers to your Pinterest profile.

You need an Administrator login to install a new plug-in. If you don't have it, ask whoever is at an Administrator level to either follow these instructions for you or provide you with administrative privileges in your WordPress site.

A few different plug-ins are available for this purpose, and all seem pretty similar. I experimented with a few before settling on the Pinterest RSS Widget as having the best features and being the least glitchy.

Here are instructions on adding the Pinterest RSS Widget plug-in to your WordPress site (although if you choose to use a different Pinterest widget plug-in, the instructions are very similar):

1. **Go to your WordPress site's backend Dashboard (usually found at** `http://yourdomainhere.com/wp-admin`**).**

2. **On the left menu, mouse over Plug-ins and click Add New (see Figure 7-4).**

The Install Plug-ins page appears and defaults to the Search tab so that you can easily find a new plug-in.

3. **Type** Pinterest RSS Widget **in the search box (as seen in Figure 7-5) and click the Search Plug-ins button.**

   WordPress returns a list of matching results from the plug-ins database.

Figure 7-4:
Clicking the Add New plug-in option.

Mouse over plug-ins

Figure 7-5:
Searching for the Pinterest RSS Widget plug-in.

4. Find the name Pinterest RSS Widget and click the Install Now linkable text.

A box pops up to confirm that you want to install this plug-in (see Figure 7-6).

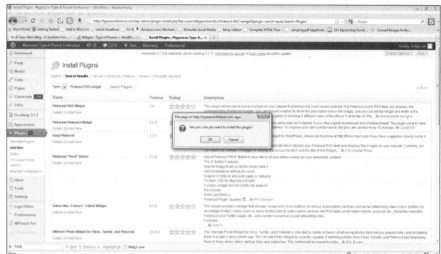

Figure 7-6:
Confirming
the plug-in
installation.

5. Click OK to continue installing the plug-in.

The Installing Plug-in page appears. After the plug-in is installed successfully, you see two links: Activate Plug-in and Return to Plug-in Installer.

6. Click the Activate Plug-in text link.

This takes you to a page listing all of your plug-ins.

7. Mouse over Appearance in the left menu and click Widgets.

This takes you to your Widgets page. The main part of this page is labeled Available Widgets and lists all the widgets you currently have installed.

8. Find Pinterest RSS Widget, and then click and drag it to place it in your sidebar.

The right side of the Widgets page shows your sidebar options. You can choose where you would like to place the Pinterest widget and simply drag it there. Figure 7-7 shows that I placed mine under an existing widget I created called "Conference Sponsors."

The Pinterest RSS Widget box expands to display the options for the widget.

9. **Enter your Pinterest username and fill out any other fields on this widget form (see Figure 7-8).**

   These fields are optional, so you can complete only those you want to use. You can experiment with different settings (different thumbnail and Follow Me button sizes or different numbers of recent pins, for example).

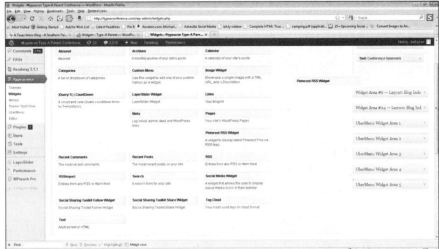

Figure 7-7:
Dragging the Pinterest RSS Widget where you want it on your site.

Figure 7-8:
Entering the settings for the Pinterest RSS Widget.

10. Click Save and review your new widget.

Check to ensure the placement is correct. You can return to Appearance⇨Widgets to tweak your options until you're happy with the result.

TIP

You can track the effectiveness of your on-site promotions of your Pinterest account if you use an analytics program with data on outbound clicks, such as Clicky (www.getclicky.com). Find out more about tracking and statistics in Chapter 11.

Promoting your Pinterest profile in your e-mail marketing

E-mail newsletters and e-blasts are another great way to find people already highly interested in your business or brand and nudge them to connect with you on Pinterest.

Here are a few ways you can nudge people to follow you in your e-mail newsletter:

✔ **Add an icon for Pinterest that links to your account (see Figure 7-9).** If you already have a spot with either text or icons (or both) for your social network presences, add Pinterest where those are located.

✔ **Include a blurb in your newsletter announcing your Pinterest page with a link to your profile, and a strong call to action to click the link and follow you.** You may even want to include a screenshot of your profile page or a Pinterest logo.

Figure 7-9: Kraft's e-mail newsletter includes a Pinterest icon at the top right.

✔ **Send a dedicated e-mail blast inviting people to connect on your Pinterest page.**

Because most e-mail marketing services provide tracking of clicks in e-mail newsletters, you can easily track interest in the Pinterest account by viewing data such as the number of clicks, who clicked, how many ultimately followed after clicking over, and so on.

MailChimp, an online e-mail marketing company, also offers a direct Pinterest integration for customers. This allows you to send a Pinterest-specific e-mail blast that includes your latest pins. If you don't already use MailChimp for your e-mail services, check your own service provider to see if they do something similar. You can also join MailChimp for free with a list of fewer than 5,000 subscribers. Before you begin the instructions below, you will need a MailChimp account, which you can get at `http://mailchimp.com`. You also need a list of e-mail subscribers to send to, which you can import from another e-mail newsletter management system or spreadsheet.

To send a MailChimp Pinterest e-mail blast,

1. **Visit** `http://pinterest.chimplets.com.`

   This takes you to a page to enter a few basic details and choose a couple of options to generate a Pinterest e-mail blast (see Figure 7-10).

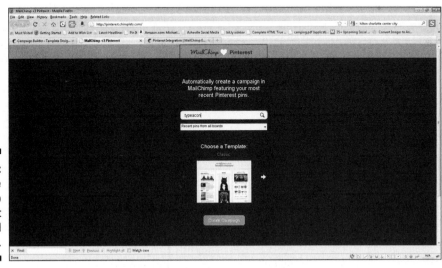

Figure 7-10: The MailChimp Pinterest e-mail generator.

2. **Enter your Pinterest profile name, choose which boards (or all) in the drop-down menu, and scroll the right and left arrows to choose a design.**

   You typically want to choose all boards, but in some situations, you might want to do an e-mail with one board (perhaps for a seasonal topic, for example).

3. **Click the Create Campaign button.**

   This takes you to a page to connect to your MailChimp account to your Pinterest account (see Figure 7-11).

4. **Enter your MailChimp log-in credentials and click the Connect button.**

   You arrive at a page to select which list to send to (you only see this option if you have more than one subscriber list). If you only have one list, skip to Step 6.

5. **Select the list and click the Done button.**

   This takes you to a page stating the e-mail has been created and is waiting in your Campaigns folder for you to modify and send.

6. **Click the Go to MailChimp button.**

   Navigate through all of the steps to create a newsletter as you normally would, paying special attention to the Edit HTML step and making sure to do a pop-up preview to see how the e-mail looks.

Check the number of Pinterest followers you have before you send the e-mail (both followers of your profile and followers for each board because anyone who follows one board won't show in your profile numbers), so you can compare afterwards to see if those who clicked through actually followed your profile.

Figure 7-11:
Connecting
to your
MailChimp
account.

7. Click the Send or Schedule button.

Your e-mail (see Figure 7-12 for a sample of the Pinterest integrated e-mail) goes into the MailChimp queue to be sent. Afterwards, you can look in your MailChimp reports to see how many subscribers opened and clicked to your Pinterest page.

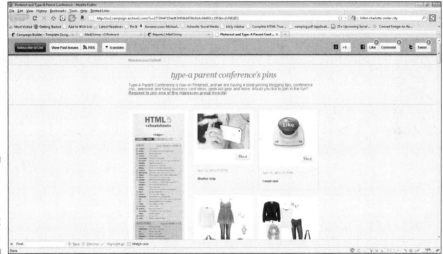

Figure 7-12:
A sample
MailChimp
Pinterest
e-mail.

Using social networks to attract Pinterest followers

People who use other social networks often use Pinterest, even though Pinterest is becoming known as the social network even your grandmother loves.

Many times, finding Pinterest members on other social networks is as simple as creating a Facebook status update, tweet or blog post announcing you are also on Pinterest, linking to your profile, and asking others to follow you.

Beyond that, you can do other things to raise awareness of your Pinterest account on other social networks. From time to time, check the Twitter and/or Facebook box when you are pinning or repinning (see details previously in Chapter 5). Or you can add Pinterest to your Facebook Timeline (which I discuss in Chapter 10).

It's helpful to know your Pinterest profile URL so you can share the link quickly and easily. You can find it by logging into Pinterest and clicking your name at the top right. You're taken to your Pinterest profile and you can copy the URL from your address bar and share it.

You can also share individual boards and pins because they also have their own URLs. To share a board, find it on your profile page. Click the image or title for the board, and that takes you to the board page. Copy the URL in the address bar and share as you see fit.

Want to quickly share a board on your Facebook profile? Navigate to the board you want to share and click the Like button at the top (shown to the right of the board name in Figure 7-13) to like a board on Facebook.

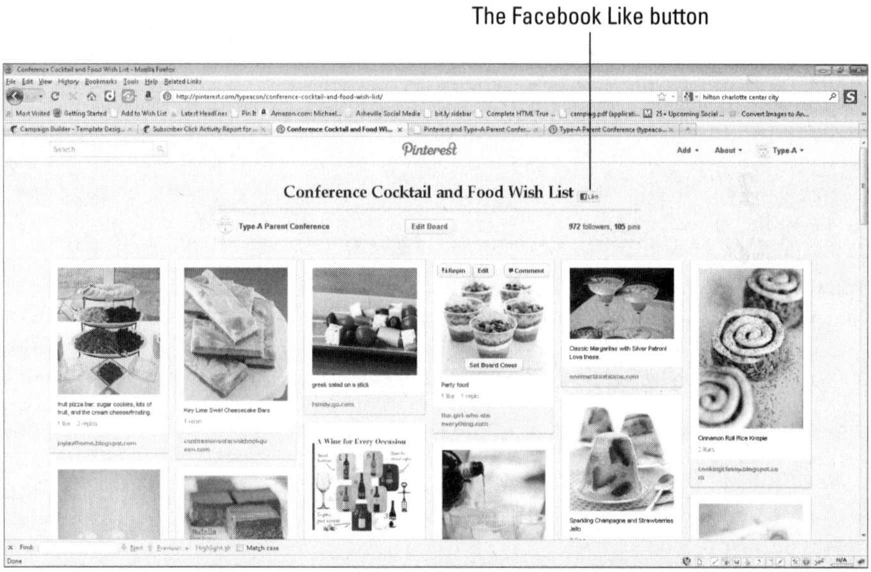

The Facebook Like button

Figure 7-13:
Clicking the
Facebook
Like button
on a board.

You can share one of your pins directly to Facebook or Twitter from the pin page by clicking the Like or Tweet buttons directly to the right of the large pin image (see Figure 7-14).

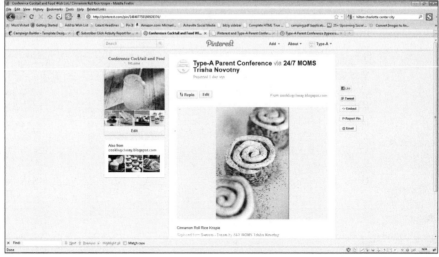

Figure 7-14:
Using the Like and Tweet buttons on a pin page.

Integrating Pinterest into Print and Broadcast Marketing Efforts

There are many places to seek out Pinterest friends beyond the usual suspects online. Be sure to include Pinterest in all of your advertising and marketing efforts and materials in broadcast and print.

It can be as simple as a small P icon on a business card to alert people that you're on Pinterest. It can be as large as a massive "Follow us on Pinterest at pinterest.com/*USERNAME*" on your billboards. For radio, a quick "Find us on Pinterest" only takes two to three seconds of airtime, and you can add a Pinterest icon and the URL of your profile at the end of a commercial or along the bottom of one.

You can find print-friendly Pinterest logos in .EPS format by visiting Pinterest, clicking About in the top menu, and clicking Press in the left menu (see Figure 7-15). Be sure to scroll down to the Artwork section to find the icons.

Figure 7-15:
Pinterest
provides
web- and
print-friendly
logo images.

TIP

If you have the space or airtime to do it, I recommend telling people exactly where to find you rather than a general "find us on Pinterest." Although this isn't always doable with your specifications or time limits, it makes people much more likely to connect with you. If they have to search, they can quickly become distracted by other results. It is also possible (even likely in some cases) they might get confused by similarly-named profiles, or misspell your name when they search. They might even search your business name, but you use a personal name.

Another option is to create a landing page to send people and include the URL for that page in all your marketing materials. The landing page should include links to all of your social profiles, such as a Connect or Social page. If you can keep it simple, such as *YOURDOMAIN*.COM/social, it will be easy for people to remember and manually enter in their browsers' address bars.

Attracting Pinterest Followers at Your Store or Location

People who use Pinterest do occasionally venture out into the wilds of IRL (in real life). You might be surprised how many customers in your stores or clients who come by your office would love to find out you are on Pinterest, too.

There are many ways to let people know they can follow you on Pinterest, such as

✔ Putting your Pinterest profile's URL on all of your receipts.

✔ Signage with a prominent Pinterest logo to alert people you are on the site.

✔ Flyers and postcards set out or dropped in customers' bags, either devoted entirely to promoting your Pinterest page or mentioning the Pinterest page.

✔ Business cards with a Pinterest icon and URL to your profile.

✔ Promotions to encourage people to take photos of their favorite products and pin them. (I cover Pinterest campaigns in more detail in Chapter 10.)

A QR code is another way to make it easy for people to find you online while in a physical location. A QR code is similar to a UPC code, and can be scanned to provide a smartphone with information or to pull up a web page.

Many people don't have smartphones or, if they do, don't have a QR code scanner downloaded onto their phone. Even some who have both just aren't inclined to scan codes. Although QR codes are fun and exciting to use, always remember to also provide a way for those who don't scan to find your Pinterest profile or social landing page by providing the URL.

Although I wouldn't recommend relying exclusively on QR codes, you can supplement any print signs or materials referring to your Pinterest with a QR code for those who like to scan them. If you are a regular QR code scanner, it is a fast and easy way to get information quickly in a real-life setting.

You can find several QR code generators online, and all are easy to use. I recommend QR Stuff at `http://qrstuff.com`, particularly their premium memberships (ranging from $3.95 for a 24-hour membership to $85.95 for a year as of this writing). Although you can use it for free, to generate a large format file for printing, you need a premium subscription. That is the case with many code generators.

To get a printer-friendly QR code at QR Stuff:

1. **Visit** `http://qrstuff.com` **and register or log in.**

   You are taken to the main page where you can generate a QR code.

2. Under 1, be sure Website URL is selected (see Figure 7-16).

Enter your Pinterest profile URL (format `http://pinterest.com/` `USERNAME`) under 2. Here, you can also choose to use a trackable link and, if you are a premium member, you can return later to get click statistics. Under 3, you can set various preferences such as DPI (set high for print) and the color of the code.

3. Click the Download button to get your image file.

Alternately, you can click Print to generate a PDF that can be used with Avery sticker printer sheets. Your image file or PDF can be used to incorporate a QR code directly linking to your Pinterest profile in print materials.

Whether you use a QR code or not, you will want to give people a true URL they can enter to visit your Pinterest profile. If you want to get a sense of how interested people are (and how successful your on-location promotion of your Pinterest profile is), you can create a trackable link to use in print.

There are also several link shorteners with tracking options, but I recommend Bitly (`http://bitly.com`) as one of the more reliable.

Bitly links typically are in the format `bit.ly/XXXXX`. You can use the automatically generated URL with random characters after `bit.ly` or you can customize what comes after the slash. If you want the link to be branded to you (and not `bit.ly`), they also offer the option to use your own short domain to shorten your URLs. You need to hire a web coder or know your way around code well enough to be able to change the DNS settings for a domain you own if you want to personalize your links.

Figure 7-16:
Generating
a code at
QR Stuff.

A registration at Bitly is free and well worth doing before you begin sharing your Pinterest link (or any other links) so you can have a record of all your trackable links for future reference. To create a shortened, trackable Bitly link,

1. **Visit** `http://bitly.com` **and register or log in.**

   You see the default link-generating page.

2. **Enter the URL for your Pinterest profile (format** `http://pinterest. com/USERNAME`**) and click the Shorten button (see Figure 7-17).**

3. **If you want custom text after the slash, click the Customize button.**

   A text box appears.

4. **Enter your customized text (do not use spaces or odd characters) and click Customize.**

5. **To use the new shortened URL, click Copy and paste it where you want to share it.**

   The URL goes onto your clipboard, and you can paste it anywhere.

To check your customized URL's statistics (meaning how often it was clicked), return to `http://bitly.com/` on the list, and click the Info Page link.

Figure 7-17:
Creating a shortened, trackable link with Bitly.

Participating in Pinterest-Related Content and Link Lists on Other Sites

One way to gain followers and engagement with your Pinterest profile is to find places off of Pinterest to share your pins, boards, or profile. Such places are known as Pinterest *linkups,* and they're becoming more popular as Pinterest grows in usage. There are linkups that are weekly as well as ones that are general or specific to a topic.

An example of a weekly linkup is one from `www.5minutesformom.com` featuring pins or boards. You can also find linkups to share Pinterest profiles. Some regular linkups allow you to share posts you would like others to pin to Pinterest.

Here are a few linkups where you can share your profile, Pinterest pins and boards, or posts you would like pinned:

✔ You can find the weekly Pin It Friday linkup at 5 Minutes for Mom (best used by businesses that are mom-owned) at `www.5minutesformom.com/category/feature-columns/pin-it-friday`.

✔ My site features a Pinterest Profile Linkup for parents at `www.typeaparent.com/pinterest-profile-linkup.html` as well as regular topic and category linkups that can be found at `www.typeaparent.com/tag/pinterest`.

✔ You can find a weekly Friday linkup, Get Pinspired, at She Promotes at `www.shepromotes.com/tag/pinterest`.

✔ At Crafty Mama of 4, you can find the Pin Me! weekly Pinterest linkup, where you can share posts you would like linked at `www.craftymamaof4.com/tag/pinterest`.

You can search Google for terms like "Pinterest linkup," "Pinterest link up," "Pinterest blog hop," or "Pinterest linky" to find more linkups, or add a topic to the search to find niche Pinterest linkups. Although there are several linkups now, I expect many more will soon be created.

Chapter 8

Engaging on Pinterest

. . . .

In This Chapter

▶ Understanding the engaging features available on Pinterest

▶ Creating a pin that encourages repins, likes, and comments

▶ Dealing with the negative and the crazy

. . . .

*T*o truly be effective and make an impact on Pinterest, you should be an integral part of the community. This is a place to build rapport with others. It takes time and effort to do that, but the results make it well worth it.

There are some concrete results from engaging on Pinterest, such as a traffic boost on your blog or website as more people share your content and repin images from your site. There are also less tangible — but equally significant — results from engaging on Pinterest. You build goodwill, affinity, and loyalty among those you engage with on Pinterest, for example.

Understanding What Is Engaging on Pinterest

It is so basic and fundamental: You should *engage* on social networks. Honestly, it is so simple it must be obvious, right? Yet this is the most common mistake by businesses, brands, nonprofits, and organizations that I see on Pinterest and other social networks.

I believe the cause of the problem is an unhealthy attachment to traditional marketing methods. What might help is to imagine all of the fundamentals of marketing — controlling the message, for example — and make up your mind that all of those fundamentals must prove themselves worthy in this new media world.

In this new world, people want to interact and they want to know they are being heard. If they are not being heard, they find your competitor who listens and answers best. That is the bottom line.

Here are the main methods of engagement on Pinterest:

- ✔ **Pinning:** This is the most basic way of engaging on Pinterest. Don't just promote your own content, but showcase content from others as well.

- ✔ **Liking:** You should be regularly clicking the like button for pins, and this is particularly useful for pins that don't rise to the level of repinning but are interesting.

- ✔ **Repinning:** This is a core activity on Pinterest, and probably the most common way members interact.

- ✔ **Following:** Yes, following. You don't just want to collect followers. You need to follow people, especially those who follow you and interact with you. No one likes a member who follows a tiny percentage of those who follow her.

- ✔ **Commenting:** This is how you communicate directly with other pinners. You won't have time (or the desire) to comment on every pin you see, but you will want to regularly comment when you have something to add.

- ✔ **Mentioning:** If you see a pin that interests a friend on Pinterest, or you are sharing a great post by a Pinterest friend, you can @ them to draw their attention to it — and to send people to their profile.

- ✔ **Sharing:** You can also share pins you make as well as interesting ones you see on social networks like Twitter and Facebook.

To be highly engaging, you should be doing all of these (and not simply picking one or two). See Figure 8-1 for an example of a pin with a variety of engagement types.

As you use Pinterest, consider what level of engagement you are using. There are varying degrees, and the best Pinterest results come from maximum engagement. The good news is that maximum engagement is much more about the style of your usage of Pinterest than the time devoted to it. Here are three levels of engagement I am assigning types to, and you should aim ideally at the top level, Engager:

- ✔ **Broadcaster.** This is the lowest level of engagement, and unfortunately quite common with business and brand accounts on Pinterest. It is characterized by only sharing pins of self-promotional content, and "Pin It to Win It" marketing campaigns (see Chapter 10 for more on that). Broadcasters have followers but they follow very few.

  If you are a popular enough brand, you can get away with being a broadcaster (especially if you have amazing content that is highly shareable) and still drive a lot of traffic to your website, but I would argue you aren't using Pinterest to its potential and you aren't gaining many of the less tangible benefits such as humanizing your brand and building a rapport with your customers. The Martha Stewart Pinterest account is a classic example of a broadcaster profile, following just 40 people compared to being followed by 35,000 users and pinning content only from Martha Stewart sites (see Figure 8-2).

✔ **Talker.** The talker does some engaging, but it is limited to repinning other people's content, a little commenting and the occasional like. They share some content that has nothing to do with promoting their brand, but most of their pins are either directly linking to their site or linking to content related to their products.

✔ **Engager.** The engager gets it, following people back, pinning and repinning content from other sites instead of only self-promoting, and creating entire boards dedicated to promoting others or sharing great content. The engager consistently uses all of the points of engagement mentioned earlier, and strives to find creative, innovative ways to market on Pinterest without turning followers off.

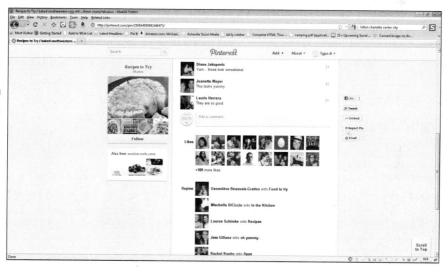

Figure 8-1: A pin with various types of engagement, including likes, comments, and repins.

Best of all, the Engager does it all while still maintaining and reinforcing the brand voice. The Engager manages to promote others, share amazing content, interact and engage, all while keeping the conversation closely tied to what the brand passion and message is. A great example is Cabot Cheese (`http://Pinterest.com/cabotcheese`). The Cabot account follows members back, has fun boards like Moo! and <3 Vermont, and shares dairy recipes from many sources (see Figure 8-3). They make following the Cabot Cheese's account fun.

Figure 8-2:
The Martha
Stewart
Pinterest
account is
an example
of a Broad-
caster.

Figure 8-3:
Cabot
Cheese is
an example
of an
Engager on
Pinterest.

Creating a Pin That Will Get Repinned

Another key factor of engagement is simply being interesting. If you consistently pin fabulous content, you get repinned and you get followers.

This starts with having great pins, whether they are pins from your site or others, or even finding the most interesting pins on Pinterest to repin. The term "interesting" is subjective, however, and it's different for each member of Pinterest. That means you need to determine what is interesting to your followers and audience.

Many times, it takes experimentation. While I mention earlier in Chapter 6 the types of pins that are popular, what is popular and effective for you depends on your followers.

Some basic properties are common to popular, highly repinned pins:

- ✔ **The image is spectacular.** Pinterest behavior is very impulsive and reactive. People browse the pins, and the most beautiful and captivating images jump off the screen.

- ✔ **The pin sparks an emotional response.** Cute animals, inspirational quotes, hilarious joke posters — these are all pins that do well and for a reason. When you see the image, you respond in some way. Figure 8-4 shows an image of a returning soldier seeing his baby for the first time. I repinned a pin of that image months ago, and I still see the image making the rounds on Pinterest simply because it evokes such an emotional response.

- ✔ **The subject of the image is unique, innovative, unusual or quirky. New technology does well, and clever handmade items do as well.** If it is something you don't see every day, it can stand out.

- ✔ **The pin shares important information.** Pins such as infographics and those connected to posts with tutorials and how-tos do very well. People tend to like and repin these to find later, and they get shared a lot.

- ✔ **The pin is about Pinterest or social media.** People active on Pinterest love to talk about Pinterest. They also are frequently active on Twitter, Facebook, Google+, and any number of other social networks (as well as blogs). Great content about Pinterest and social media performs well.

To experiment and see what works best for your Pinterest account, share a variety of pin types on a mix of topics and occasionally throw in one that is a little different.

Keep an eye on your pins to see which ones generate a lot of repins. You can do that by visiting your profile page and clicking the Pins link to see your latest pins (in reverse chronological order). With each pin thumbnail, you also see statistics on likes and repins, and the latest comments (see Figure 8-5).

One benefit of creating pins that generate interaction is that you are more likely to land on Pinterest's Popular page. Pinterest has not officially explained how to land on that page, but it appears to be a combination of factors that include the number of repins, likes, and comments.

Figure 8-4:
An image
that has
been popu-
lar as a pin
on Pinterest.

Figure 8-5:
On your
profile pin
page, you
can see
statistics on
interactions
with your
pins.

Pin statistics

Creating a Pin That Encourages Comments

Commenting provides a chance for you to get feedback and virtually network
with your followers.

Getting comments can be a challenge. Don't be discouraged if the lion's share
of your pins get no comments. This is actually pretty common for most users.

The main exception is users with tens of thousands of followers, who get repins and comments on many of their pins.

Still, that is no reason to give up hope! A heavily commented pin drives attention to the pin and to your profile. Any commenter who has e-mail notifications set to receive a message for follow-up comments can return to the pin as more people comment.

You can spark comments in a few ways, but again, none of this is universal. There is no guarantee that if you make a pin that fits into this list that you will get overwhelmed with an outpouring of comments. These are some tips related to which types of pins spark conversation:

- ✔ **Controversial pins:** For many people, the trade-off isn't worth it because you can alienate many followers and end up with rude comments and personal attacks among commenters. If you are running a Pinterest profile for a political campaign or a cause, however, this could be a great strategy to get people into the conversation.

- ✔ **Lovely pins:** Travel, food, and pretty craft pins get comments, sometimes of people saying they have been there, done that. Other times, people simply declare their approval.

- ✔ **Pins that make you go "aww!":** Cute pins bring out the commenters — they just can't resist saying how adorable a baby, kitten, or wild animal is. Think I'm kidding? See Figure 8-6, a picture of a pig in rain boots that got 25 comments (not to mention more than 730 likes and 3,500 repins).

Again, there are no rules about what is effective. You should experiment, and when you have a pin that gets a lot of comments, make note of it. This helps you determine which pins get your followers talking.

Figure 8-6:
Cute pins
tend to
attract
commenters.

Handling Trolls, Spammers, and Negative or Inappropriate Interaction

For the most part, Pinterest is new and the amount of bad behavior is pretty low. Still, I've run a social network myself for five years and I know that you can never guarantee a 100 percent spam-free, attack-free, junk-free space. Someone always slips in and annoys or offends others.

If you have a single comment that is offensive, you can mouseover the comment on the pin page and click the X that appears to the right to remove it. I would caution you against doing this for every comment that isn't full of sunshine, however (for example, healthy debate or a minor complaint or concern). It is best to remove comments only when they are attacking, hateful or obscene. Otherwise, attacks on your company can escalate and move to other social networks.

You can also report any pin as spam, porn, hateful, or otherwise inappropriate. My personal experience, and what I have heard from others, is that Pinterest responds very quickly (sometimes within minutes) to reported pins.

To report a pin:

1. **Go to the pin page and click the Report Pin button to the right of the image (see Figure 8-7).**

   A window pops up, listing a number of possible reasons for reporting the pin.

2. **Select the reason for the report, such as nudity or graphic violence, and click the Report Pin button (see Figure 8-8).**

   Selecting Other brings up a box to let you explain why you are reporting the pin. If you are reporting a pin because the image is a copyright violation, click the text link to use a different process for that.

   After you click Report Pin, a window pops up stating that Pinterest will review the pin and remove it if it violates Pinterest Terms of Service.

Occasionally, people get rowdy on your pins, perhaps leaving rude comments. *Trolls* are people who use websites and forums to post inflammatory comments with the express purpose of provoking people. Other times, discussions simply get heated. People also tend to be more snarky and snide online, where they don't have to say these statements to anyone's face.

Click to report a pin

Figure 8-7:
Finding the
Report Pin
button.

Figure 8-8:
The options
when you
report a pin.

Here are some tips for dealing with heated debates, rude comments, and trolls:

- ✔ **Keep your cool.** I recommend that to anyone online, but it is even more crucial if you are on Pinterest for marketing purposes. Believe me, no one looks good in an Internet showdown. This doesn't mean you have to be a pushover. Be firm, but be civil and polite. You want to be the one who rises above it.

- ✔ **Let it remain if it isn't a personal attack on you or someone else.** It might be tempting, if someone posts a comment with the slightest hint of negativity, to delete that pin and shove your head in the sand. On other platforms, companies have made this mistake. When you silence someone with legitimate negative feedback, you often prompt a massive attack from many people. Instead, publicly respond nicely and give people a way to connect off the public venue by sharing an e-mail address. In fact, after you get past being offended, you may realize you just received important customer feedback.

- ✔ **Recognize the difference between a troll and someone genuinely upset.** That is easier said than done. A troll will often continuously comment on your various pins or posts (and may follow you to your own site and other social networks), seeking you out specifically. If you continue to have issues with one member, send an e-mail to hi@pinterest.com and report the issue.

Being a Good Pinterest Citizen

Pinterest is a community, just like a real-world community in a sense. There are standards for behavior, and there are people who do more contributing versus people who do more taking. To best represent your organization, you want to be an active and supportive member of the community.

One way to do that is to help keep Pinterest as it is now, relatively spam-free. When you do see spam, don't just shake your head; instead, use the Report Pin button mentioned earlier in this chapter.

Don't be an annoying, overly self-promotional, anti-social, or a "gimme" type of member. Follow the etiquette mentioned in Chapter 2. Simply following those guidelines goes a long way to being viewed as a valuable member of the Pinterest community.

Primarily, think of ways to help your fellow members and to promote them, not yourself. Although I realize that sounds counter-productive to using Pinterest for marketing purposes, you will be surprised at how powerful that is. In the long run, people remember who helped them and who supported them and they usually return the favor without being asked.

Chapter 9

Creating Pin-Worthy Content

In This Chapter

▶ Finding out who has already pinned your site

▶ Optimizing your images for Pinterest

▶ Dealing with misuse of your images

A fascinating side-effect of Pinterest is that it highlights the need for a business or brand to have great content. I know many businesses have been leaning towards putting some (or all) of their attention online to sites like Facebook. All along, I have argued that your own site (and especially your own steady flow of content on your blog) is the core of your online and social media efforts. Yes, be on Facebook, be on Twitter, but not while abandoning your own site and blog.

It is like having ornaments and no Christmas tree. Sure, the ornaments are shiny and pretty, but you've got nothing to hang them on. Pinterest has a way of really drawing attention to businesses' need for great content that is pin-worthy.

Take a moment and think about whether your site or blog has anything pin-worthy. If it doesn't, making it more shareable is going to have implications far beyond better buzz on Pinterest.

Finding Your Content That Has Been Shared on Pinterest

You might already have buzz on Pinterest before you even signed up or bought this book. Of course, this is all the more reason to get involved in Pinterest. Your business or brand may already be talked about on Pinterest (positively or negatively), and you want to know about it.

To find pins linking to your site or blog, type `http://pinterest.com/source/YOURDOMAIN.COM` into your browser's address bar, replacing *YOURDOMAIN.COM* with your site's domain. This takes you to a page of results pinned from your site (see Figure 9-1).

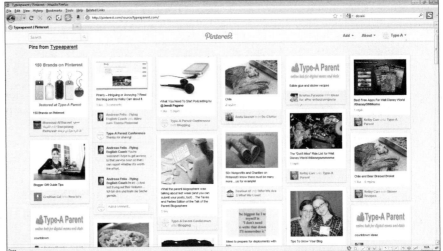

Figure 9-1:
A page of
pins from
a specific
domain.

This doesn't show everyone who has pinned and repinned your content as separate thumbnails, but instead just the original sources. You can click on any pin, however, to see who repinned at the bottom (see Figure 9-2). In fact, you can go down the rabbit hole and keep doing this with people's pins and repins until your head spins. Just be aware that the results on this page only reflect original pins, not repins, so are just a snapshot of the buzz you are getting. A great way to figure out which pin drives the most traffic is to examine your website or blog statistics, which I cover in detail in Chapter 11. In fact, seeing massive traffic referrals from Pinterest is what has driven many businesses to check out the site and is the first way many hear of the site.

Figure 9-2:
Finding a
list of who
repinned a
pin at the
bottom of a
pin page.

You can also see all pins from a particular domain from a pin page that used that domain as its source. Each pin page shows the source if it has a link connected to it.

To find the domain page from a pin,

1. **Visit the pin page and scroll down to the bottom right where it says Pinned From via [source type, typically web] from [domain.com] (see Figure 9-3).**

Figure 9-3:
Finding the
source
of a pin.

2. **Where you see the domain name, click it (it's a text link).**

   This takes you to the results page for pins from that domain.

Making It Easy to Pin Your Images

If you find that people are already pinning images from your site, great, but it's nothing to panic over if they haven't yet. The first step to seeing it happen (or to seeing your pins increase) is to make it easy for people to pin images from your site.

Adding the Pin It web button

On any site, you can add the Pinterest Pin It web button code. I prefer some of the options available on WordPress, so if you use that platform, skip these instructions and go to the "Adding a WordPress Pin It Plug-in" section later in this chapter. The downside to the instructions for adding the Pin It web button is that you must manually add code to each page you want the Pin It button to appear on. This can be a major issue if you have a lot of posts or a large online catalog.

If you don't use WordPress, it may be worth the investment to hire your web developer or a coder to create an option to universally add a Pin It button throughout your site. As Pinterest gains popularity, some other platforms will likely also offer add-ons, modules, and plug-ins for this purpose, so check before you hire a developer. Also Google for "[*platform name*] Pinterest" to see if one exists, and perhaps even add that as a Google Alert so you find out if one is announced.

To add the Pinterest Pin It button for websites, follow these steps:

1. **From the Pinterest home page, mouse over the About link and, from the drop-down menu that appears, click Pin It Button.**

   The Goodies page appears.

2. **Scroll down the page and locate the Pin It Button for Websites section. (See Figure 9-4.)**

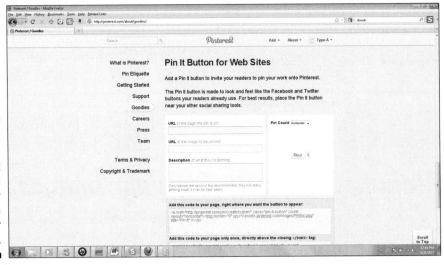

Figure 9-4: The Pinterest instructions and code for adding a Pin It button for websites.

3. **Find and copy the URL for the blog post, article, or web page you will add the code to.**

   The URL should be the deep link (or *permalink*) to that web page, not your site's home page (unless your home page is the page you're adding the button to). You can usually find the permalink for an article by clicking the title.

4. **Paste the URL in the URL of the Webpage the Pin Is On field.**

5. **Find and copy the URL for the image you want people to pin that's located on the page.**

   On the page, you can find the URL for the image on a PC by right-clicking and viewing the image or right-clicking and viewing the image URL, and then copying. On a Mac, you can get the image URL by pressing Ctrl while clicking the image and then choosing Copy Image Location from the options that appear.

6. **Paste the image URL into the URL of the Image to Be Pinned field.**

7. **(Optional) Type a description of the pin in the Description text box.**

   A clear description here is optimal. If you include a description, this will automatically be populated when a user pins that image.

8. **(Optional) Use the drop-down menu in the right column to choose between a horizontal or vertical button or to display without a pin count.**

9. **Copy the code you see in the Add This Code to Your Site text box.**

10. **Paste the code in the source (not visual) editor for your page or post where you want it to appear.**

    The best locations are above and below content (or both) or right next to, above, or below the image you would like pinned. You will also need to include the JavaScript code on this page (or universally on all pages) for the pin button to work. You need the JavaScript code just once on a page, but you can create multiple pin it buttons if you have several images on the page.

Adding a WordPress Pin It plug-in

If you have a WordPress site, you have a much wider variety of options when it comes to Pin It buttons. Although a number of plug-ins offer the option to add a Pin It button, they are all still relatively new and I have found many are buggy. I provide instructions here for some options, but also keep an eye out for newer plug-ins by searching the WordPress site at http://wordpress.org/extend/plugins/.

The main choices are to install a social sharing plug-in that includes Pinterest or a solo Pinterest sharing plug-in. The advantage of a social sharing plug-in is that you can give people options for multiple social networks, such as Facebook, Twitter, and Google+, along with Pinterest all in one place. The downside is the combo plug-ins don't always have as many options for Pinterest specifically, and I found in testing that some flat out don't work properly for Pinterest. Too many social sharing options also can clutter your design and overwhelm a visitor with too many choices.

A solo Pinterest Pin It plug-in typically gives you much more control over encouraging sharing on Pinterest, but it doesn't always play well displaying alongside other social sharing buttons (and could require code tweaking or help from a web designer). That isn't an issue if you only want to display a Pinterest button and no other social networks, but then you lose the potential sharing on those sites.

If you already have a social sharing plug-in of some sort, you might want to peek at its settings again (or see if it needs an update) to see if it has a Pinterest button included. Several of the social sharing plug-ins, including Digg Digg, Sharing Is Caring, Social Sharing Toolkit, and Really Simple Social Facebook Twitter Share Buttons, have added a Pinterest option.

If you wish to have only a Pinterest Pin It button, a number of plug-ins exist for that purpose. Although I recommend including sharing buttons for at least Twitter, Facebook, Google+, and Pinterest, there are some reasons to use a stand-alone Pin It plug-in. For example, you might want to manually place a Pin It button right before or after each image. You might also wish to place a Pin It button in a different location than your other sharing buttons.

I have found issues with essentially every plug-in related to social sharing, so I will share instructions for the one I recommend most.

Whichever plug-in you choose, be sure to test it thoroughly once you deploy it live. You should check how it appears on your home page if you opt to display it there for a blog format (conflicts with themes are common). You should check the appearance on the posts or pages. Also test by doing a few pins from your site, and then visiting the pin pages to examine them, click to be sure they lead to your domain, the images on the pin page show full size and not in thumbnail size, and so on.

I discovered issues with a few plug-ins and I had to disable them as a result. For example, popular social sharing plug-in Digg Digg initially had a major issue when adding Pinterest to the buttons: no image was pulled into the pin. When they fixed it, I noticed a new issue replaced it. Instead of pinning the full-size image, Digg Digg pins a very small and not Pinterest-optimized thumbnail image (if your theme uses thumbnails). I encountered similar issues with a few plug-ins, as well as an issue in which only your featured image for a post (if set) could be used.

I have found that at the time of this writing, Really Simple Social Facebook Twitter Share Buttons is one that pins full size images instead of thumbnails. Because image optimization is crucial on Pinterest, I am including instructions for that plug-in. Things change quickly as plug-ins update, so I recommend comparing and testing the plug-ins available at the time you read this.

To add a Pinterest button as part of a package of social sharing icons, you can install Really Simple Social Facebook Twitter Share Buttons with these instructions:

1. **Go to the dashboard of your WordPress site and log in.**

   The URL is typically `http://YOURDOMAIN.COM/wp-admin`.

2. **Under the Plug-ins menu, click Add New.**

   The Install Plug-ins page appears.

3. **In the Search Plug-ins text box, type** Really Simple Social Facebook Twitter Share Buttons **and then click the Search button.**

   WordPress returns a list of results.

4. **Find the result for Really Simple Social Facebook Twitter Share Buttons and click the Install Now link.**

   A pop-up window appears and asks whether you're sure you want to install this plug-in.

5. **Click OK.**

   The Installing Plug-in page appears and installs the plug-in on your site.

6. **Click the Activate Plug-in link to make the plug-in live on your site.**

   You return to your main Plug-ins page.

7. **Find the Settings menu in your WordPress admin menu (usually in the left column or at the top of the page), and click Really Simple Share in the submenu.**

   The options page for the plug-in appears.

8. **Set your options.**

   • Indicate whether to include a counter to display the number of shares for each social network (see Figure 9-5).

   • Check the box for each social network button you wish to include, and you can drag each box up or down to rearrange the display order.

   • You can also set certain Twitter settings. I recommend including your Twitter username here if you have one so tweets will reference your account with an @.

   • Under Show Buttons in These Pages, select at least Pages and Posts. You want to test all other visibility options because they are pages that typically show snippets of multiple pages and those can appear wonky.

Figure 9-5:
Setting your
options for
the Really
Simple
Share
plug-in.

9. Click the Save Changes button at the bottom of the page.

Now visit your site, posts, and pages to confirm that the share buttons
appear properly, and that they work when clicked and submitted. You should
see the buttons you checked appearing and, if your posts have had any
shares (even before the installation), you should see a number next to each if
you checked the counter option (see Figure 9-6).

These numbers show how many times your pin has been shared.

Figure 9-6:
The Really
Simple
Share plug-
in on a site.

Another option is to get a plug-in that only adds a pin button and does not add buttons for any other social networks. A few stand-alone plug-ins do this. The main issue I have encountered in trying them all is that they can be buggy, much like the social sharing plug-ins with multiple networks, and that they don't function as I would like.

Installing the Pinterest "Pin It" Button plug-in

The standalone Pin It button plug-in I recommend is the Pinterest "Pin It" Button plug-in. You can see details at `http://wordpress.org/extend/plugins/pinterest-pin-it-button` for the plug-in (see Figure 9-7). It has a wide variety of options. You can set your image to be pinned or let the user set it, for example. You can automatically place the button above and below content and on various types of pages or posts, or you can use a short code to manually add it where you want or place it in a sidebar widget. *Short code* is a snippet of code, usually in brackets, that automatically renders something on a page, post, or widget. The developer offers more Pinterest plug-ins at `http://pinterestplugin.com`.

To install this plug-in, follow these steps:

1. **Go to the dashboard of your WordPress site and log in.**

   The URL is typically `http://YOURDOMAIN.COM/wp-admin`.

Figure 9-7:
The
Pinterest
"Pin It"
Button
plug-in.

2. **Under the Plug-ins menu, click Add New.**

   The Install Plug-ins page appears.

3. **In the Search Plug-ins text box, type** Pinterest Pin It Button **and then click the Search button.**

   WordPress returns a list of results.

4. **Find the result for Pinterest "Pin It" Button and click the Install Now link.**

   Note that you may see more than one result for Pinterest Pin It Button. You want to choose the one with quotes around "Pin It."

   A pop-up window appears and asks whether you're sure you want to install this plug-in.

5. **Click OK.**

   The Installing Plug-in page appears and installs the plug-in on your site.

6. **Click the Activate Plug-in link to make the plug-in live on your site.**

   You return to your main Plug-ins page.

7. **Find the Pinterest "Pin It" Button option in your WordPress admin menu (usually in the left column or at the top of the page), and click it.**

   The Pinterest "Pin It" Button Settings page appears.

8. **Set your preferences and click the Save Changes button at the bottom of the page.** From here, you have a variety of options regarding where to display the button. You can choose the types of content where the button will display (such as the homepage or individual posts) as well as the physical location of the pin when it appears on content. (See Figure 9-8.)

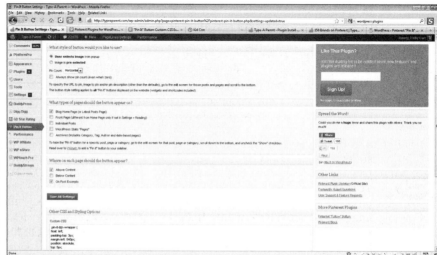

Figure 9-8:
Setting your
Pinterest
"Pin It"
Button
preferences.

9. **Visit your site as well as content types where you selected the button to appear (such as pages or posts) to be sure it appears correctly.**

10. **Click the Pin It button to be sure it works properly.**

You can also use the short code [pinit] to display a pin anywhere manually in your content. This code can be handy for content with several images, where you want to remind people to pin right before or after images. The short code also allows you to include a variety of commands, such as the image URL to be pinned (handy if you want to have each image Pin Button pin that specific image, for example).

Here is sample code that sets the style of button count, which URL to link the pin to, which URL to use for the actual image file to set which image, a pin description to pre-populate in the form and which side of the page the button should align to:

```
[pinit count="vertical" url="http://www.mysite.com"
       image_url="http://www.mysite.com/myimage.
       jpg" description="My favorite image!"
       float="right"].
```

Creating Pin-Friendly Images

The core requirement for your site to perform well on Pinterest, both by being pinned and driving traffic, is to have images (and content with them) that are optimized for Pinterest.

For many, this can be an issue if you've been using small images, such as less than 150 pixels by 150 pixels (or not at all), and have many pages or posts that are not optimized. I would make your newest, most popular, and most interesting content and images your top priority first, with a long-range goal of optimizing everything else later.

For example, if you have a blog, concentrate on including optimized images for new posts as you write them. If you have an online catalog, focus on optimizing images for your newest and hottest products first.

A quick way to test your site's image optimization, if you already have some content pinned by yourself or others, is to visit your domain's source page at http://pinterest.com/source/*YOURDOMAIN.COM* (replace *YOURDOMAIN.COM* with your domain). Click on the pins to view the full pin pages. If you see a lot of gray space to the left and right of your images (and images that are much smaller than the space), you either have images on your site that are too small for the full pin page or you have a plug-in that is pulling in a thumbnail instead of a full-sized image.

I discovered that my sites' logos (which were in a .png format) were getting badly distorted when pinned. That was important information, as my blog has some posts with no images from the archives that were being pinned (and the logo was the only image choice). Because I checked my source page, I was able to find out about it and convert my logos to .JPG format images that played better with the Pinterest system. Now any pins from articles without images at least have a nice-looking logo.

Next, be sure the image on your page is pinnable. If you use something like a plug-in (an add-on for a web platform to give it additional functionality) such as a photo gallery or lightbox plug-in to display images on a page or a post, it may prevent the image from being pinned. You can check whether the images on your page or post are pinnable by going to your page or post you wish to pin, copying the URL, and then heading over to Pinterest to create a pin manually. When you add the URL for the pin, you'll be able to see whether Pinterest can find any images to pin. I have instructions on how to create a pin in Chapter 5.

If some of the images on your page or post don't appear, it's typically because some sort of dynamic coding is being used to display your images. (You can't pin from Facebook, for example, as shown in Figure 9-9.)

Examine your site's plug-ins, add-ons, modules, or code for a feature that's used to display images. When you find it, you may need to disable the plug-in entirely or check with that plug-in's developer for a workaround. With so many possibilities — website and blog platforms and various third-party plug-ins — I can't address all possibilities with instructions in these pages.

The best bet is to go to the source, such as a support forum for your website or blog platform or for the plug-in itself, and ask whether anyone else is having this issue and has found a solution.

Figure 9-9:
You can't
pin an
image from
some sites,
such as
Facebook.

After you've verified that images on your page or post can be pinned, you need to ensure the images will display well and engage your audience on Pinterest. Here are some tips:

- **Be sure images are a minimum of 250 pixels on both sides, ideally.** Although people can pin smaller images, on Pinterest, the guideline is, "Bigger is better." An image of at least 250 pixels wide fills the space (without distortion) on mobile pin feeds, pin results pages, and as a board cover. To optimize for the pin page, your image can be as wide as 600 pixels. There is no limit on length.

- **You might consider adding a watermark to the images you own and post that you hope will be pinned.** Adding a watermark helps gain more exposure for your site's name and also protects images if they're used without your permission elsewhere. Most image-editing programs have a watermark option, and you can also find software available for the purpose of adding watermarks. The goal with a watermark is to display ownership clearly (and in a manner that makes it difficult for someone to remove your watermark) without interfering with the appearance of the image. This is why watermarks often have transparent text or logos. Some free websites allow you to watermark your images, such as www. picmarkr.com and www.watermarktool.com. If you use WordPress, you can also find plug-ins that watermark all images (Watermark RELOADED is well-rated). I include instructions for adding a watermark to images later in this chapter.

- **Consider adding text onto the image describing the content that people will find if they navigate to your site from the pin (as shown in Figure 9-10).** Adding text to an image can help encourage people to click through the image to get the information.

Figure 9-10: An image from a site that includes text stating what's in the content when you click through.

✔ **Some people also use collages (see Figure 9-11) with multiple images to show that the content is a tutorial, which can be enticing to those who see it in their Pinterest stream.** The trick here is to avoid giving it all away (otherwise, why should they click through at all?) but to demonstrate that clicking through is worthwhile for the meaty content like instructions, a tutorial, or a page with lovely images.

Figure 9-11:
A collage
to depict
multiple
images — in
this case,
steps to a
DIY post.

Handling Image Pinning Issues

You bought this book, so I am going to go out on a limb and assume you want to get on Pinterest to market your business, your website, your services, your organization, or you. That means that in most cases, you want to encourage people to pin your images. What you want to avoid, however, is misuse of your images (such as pinning without properly linking to your site or giving credit).

There may even be instances where you want to prevent certain images or all of your images from being pinned at all. You might also want to ensure images that get mis-pinned (for example, someone downloads an image from your site and then uploads it separately without linking you or attributing your site) still lead people to your site somehow with a watermark.

Watermarking your images

Watermarking and branding your images in some way, as mentioned earlier in this chapter, is the best self-defense when it comes to image theft. Even with a watermark, however, people might still embed the pins, upload the image as a pin so that it isn't connected to your site, or copy the image and use it on their own site, Facebook Timeline, or wherever they wish.

If that happens, the great thing about a watermark (unless you encounter someone really maniacal who crops the watermark out or edits the photo in some way to distort it) is that you get attribution no matter how someone uses your image. No, it isn't ideal. Yes, that is your photo for crying out loud. But it is also free advertising.

Before you watermark an image, make a copy of it first. You want to always be sure to have an original, unedited, unresized, and unwatermarked version. You might, for example, need it for marketing materials where you don't want to have a watermark.

Although lots of photo and image editors are out there, Photoshop Elements is one of the most popular and the one I chose to use for instructions. (For these instructions, I assume you have basic knowledge on how to use Photoshop.) Here is how to watermark an image in Photoshop Elements:

1. **Open Photoshop and click File⇨Open and select the image you wish to watermark.**

   The image appears on the screen.

2. **At the top menu, click Layer ⇨ New ⇨ Layer (see Figure 9-12).**

   A layer creation box pops up.

3. **Click the down arrow to the right of Opacity (see Figure 9-13).**

   Ideally, a watermark should have some transparency, so move the dial to the left to reduce the opacity. I prefer 30 percent opacity.

Figure 9-12:
Creating a
new layer in
Photoshop.

(Optional) You can also name the layer and experiment with different modes (although Normal is perfectly fine and probably preferable).

Figure 9-13:
Setting the
new layer
options.

4. **Click OK.**

5. **Click the text icon (a capital letter T) in the Tools menu (typically to the left) to switch to Text mode.**

6. **Click the color box at the bottom to set the text color (see Figure 9-14).**

   For darker images, white is ideal, and for lighter images, black is ideal.

Figure 9-14:
Setting the
text color.

7. **Click where you want the watermark to show on the image.**

8. **Type a copyright statement, your business name, your domain or a combination of those (see Figure 9-15).**

Your intent is to get the credit (and possibly traffic referrals) you desire, so when it doubt, I recommend using your domain if you only want to use a small amount of text.

You can type a copyright symbol by typing ALT+0169.

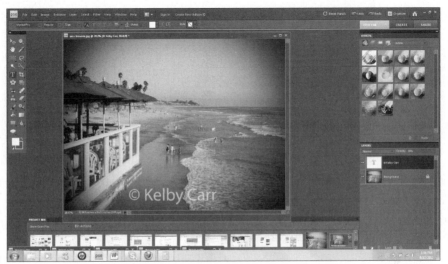

Figure 9-15: Typing your watermark text.

9. **Click File⇨Save As and name your image file. Save it in a location where it will be easy to find later for uploading onto your website.**

.JPG is typically the best format.

Reporting a copyright violation

You might one day see an image from your site that has gone viral, and you aren't benefitting in the slightest because someone uploaded it without any credit. Yep, that is frustrating. Fortunately, I have heard from several people who have reported copyright violations on Pinterest and the original pin (plus all repins) were removed rapidly.

You also may simply not wish to have your image shared (or a particular image shared) on Pinterest and be the copyright owner. Perhaps you sell the image as a photographer or artist, for example, or maybe it is a photo with your children you don't want spread like wildfire.

If that happens, this is how to report a copyright violation:

1. **From the homepage of Pinterest, mouse over About and click Copyright from the drop-down menu.**

   This takes you to a page with text about Pinterest's policy regarding copyright complaints. You also see instructions for filing a complaint in writing if you prefer to (these instructions are for filing the complaint online).

2. **Scroll down and click the red Copyright Complaint Form button (see Figure 9-16).**

Figure 9-16:
The
Pinterest
copyright
page.

3. **Enter the details in the form that appears (see Figure 9-17).**

   If you have multiple images that have been used inappropriately and/or multiple pins to report, you can click Identify Another to keep adding boxes.

4. **Click the Submit Notification button at the bottom of the page.**

   The complaint is submitted to Pinterest for review.

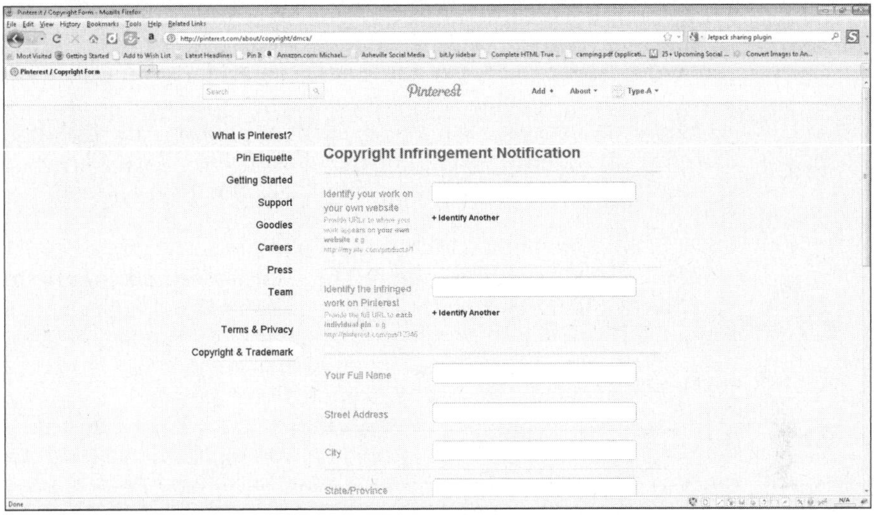

Figure 9-17:
The
Pinterest
copyright
complaint
form.

Blocking pinning of your images

As I said earlier, blocking pinning of images pretty much negates any hope of marketing on Pinterest. Still, in special cases (such as a stock photography site, for example, where the whole intent of the business is to sell images for use on websites), you may want to completely stay off Pinterest.

Pinterest makes it relatively simple to block images from pinning, so that is the good news.

For any site, you can add a snippet of code to your site's header coding to block pinning site-wide. This is the code:

```
<meta name="pinterest" content="nopin" />
```

It must go into the header code, and not anywhere else in your site's coding, to work. If you don't know how to do this, hire a web developer to do it for you. It takes a knowledgeable person mere seconds to change this code if your header is dynamically used for the whole site (as is the case with most web platforms).

To test that it works, attempt to pin an image from any page. You should see this message pop up: "This site doesn't allow pinning to Pinterest. Please contact the owner with any questions. Thanks for visiting!"

WordPress users can use a plug-in to block pinning called, naturally, Pinterest Block. Although a couple of WordPress plug-ins are available for this purpose, I find that Pinterest Block has the most options.

You can find the Pinterest Block plug-in at `http://wordpress.org/ extend/plugins/pinterest-block/` or by visiting your WordPress dashboard and mousing over Plug-ins, clicking Add Plug-in, and entering **Pinterest Block** in the search box to install. (You can find detailed instructions on adding a WordPress plug-in earlier in this chapter in the "Installing the Pinterest "Pin It" Button plug-in" section.)

Pinterest Block is handy because it lets you block all images from your site, block certain content types (for example, allowing pins from posts but blocking pins from pages), or individually block a specific page or post from being pinned.

Chapter 10

Generating Buzz on Pinterest

In This Chapter

▶ Finding your brand evangelists and reaching out to them

▶ Creating an imaginative, successful Pinterest marketing campaign

▶ Understanding the pros and cons of Pinterest contests

*P*interest can be a powerful platform for generating buzz and connecting with influencers. It can drive interest in a product launch, and it can spark conversations about your services. It is a place where you can find the people who already love and share about your product or service, and it is a place where you can find those with similar affinities and connect.

Although people get on Pinterest and share about products and services, there is a strong sense that Pinterest is a place to be creative and share beautiful things. Marketing can feel strongly like it is tainting the site. In all marketing endeavors, be mindful that you should be adding to the Pinterest experience, not taking away from it with the hard sell.

Engaging with Your Brand Enthusiasts

You very well might already have brand evangelists singing your company's praises on Pinterest right now. Don't simply make note of it in a report to your board or your boss. Talk to those people. Become their friends. If they are already enamored with your brand, imagine how much more so they will be if you engage them.

If you have a small or lesser-known business, you may not have evangelists already waiting in the wings. But even in those cases, you might be surprised.

I know bloggers who don't get tons of traffic who were surprised to find a significant number of their posts were being pinned by loyal readers. You don't have to be a household name to have fans on Pinterest (or to build up a fan base on Pinterest).

A simple way to find fans is to search for those who have pinned your products, blog posts, or site and thank them for sharing. My friend Robin Plemmons, who has an Etsy shop, Lemons with a Pea, for her artwork, has done this for some time. Figure 10-1 shows how she commented on a pin of a postcard in her catalog.

Figure 10-1:
Find pins of your site or products and thank the person for sharing.

You can find pins related to your company a few ways:

- ✔ **Use Pinterest search.** You can the search box at the top left of the site a few different ways. Search for pins with your product or company name in the description by leaving it to the default pin search. You can also search for your company name, your personal name, your product or service name, and so on. Even consider including common misspellings.

- ✔ **Use the source search to find all pins from your website in format** `http://pinterest.com/source/YOURDOMAIN.COM` **(replacing** `YOURDOMAIN.COM` **with your domain).**

- ✔ **Use Google search.** In the search box, enter **site:pinterest.com** and your search terms (such as company or product name). For example, **site:pinterest.com Lemons with a Pea.**

After you find your fans, comment and thank them for sharing. Follow them. You might even ultimately want to connect on a more advanced level, reaching out to these fans for cross-platform campaigns. For example, you might offer to pay them to be brand ambassadors or spokespeople (especially in the case of influential bloggers).

If you find haters, don't ignore them unless they are clearly trolls stirring up trouble. If someone has a complaint about your company or organization in a pin, respond and politely ask if you can help and provide a business contact e-mail address to take it offline. You might be surprised how you can turn a disgruntled customer into a rabid fan by simply listening and responding.

Although buzz from anyone is great news on Pinterest, you may also be fortunate enough to get pinned by one of Pinterest's power users (some members have hundreds of thousands of followers, even millions). When that happens, you might be amazed at the traffic referrals and impact you get. Just be aware that you can't really hound a top influencer to spread buzz about your company (they will not like it), and it should come organically.

Wondering what kind of influence a power user wields? Power user Michael Wurm (`http://pinterest.com/inspiredbycharm`) pinned an image of my book *Pinterest For Dummies.* The pin received more than 600 likes and 850 repins. He is one of the most popular members of Pinterest, with close to a million followers.

Running Successful Pinterest Marketing Campaigns

Running a successful Pinterest campaign is tricky. Pinterest is seen as a place for beauty and inspiration, so you must be careful to avoid appearing to be a commercial or a press release. You want to connect with members by making the campaign fun, interesting, and something they want to discover, not avoid.

For example, anything that requires pinning the same pin will likely annoy members quickly. Anything that looks like an ad has the same effect. The best Pinterest campaigns encourage people to do what Pinterest is used best for: to pin wonderful things they would want to share with others. The challenge is to do that while still getting marketing benefits (brand awareness, traffic, more followers, and so on) from the campaign.

Pinterest is new and marketing campaigns on Pinterest are even newer. Don't limit yourself to an idea that has already been tested. A great way to capture attention (and coverage on major sites like Mashable) is to come up with a new and clever way to engage on Pinterest.

Here are a few guidelines to provide a litmus test to your crazy, creative Pinterest marketing campaign:

✔ Will it annoy people?

✔ Will it be spammy?

✔ Would people never pin or repin this if it weren't part of a campaign with some sort of incentive?

✔ Are you asking people to do a whole lot for your brand and get little (or just a potential prize) in return?

If you answered yes to any of the above, rethink your campaign. Even though you might get some participation (and therefore, rationalize the campaign was a success), it likely wasn't worth it. This is the case in almost every Pin It to Win It campaign I have seen (more on that later in this chapter). You probably alienated as many people as you engaged, and it had the opposite of the desired effect (instead of the buzz raising positive awareness about your business, it raised awareness that was negative).

The other litmus test is whether you will gain something from the campaign. As fun as Pinterest is, you should have a goal and, ideally, a way to measure success at the end of the campaign. Ask yourself these questions:

✔ Will it raise positive awareness of my organization or brand?

✔ Will it boost public perception?

✔ Will it increase my number of Pinterest followers?

✔ Will it drive traffic to my site?

✔ Will it boost sales?

✔ Will it be a chance to experiment on Pinterest and gauge response from the public and, if so, will that help us strategically plan for our efforts there in the future?

You should answer yes to at least one of these questions, or rethink your campaign. I can't tell you which of these questions is the one that you should answer yes to — that's something you need to decide as you plan your campaign. It is okay to have more than one as your goal (or all of them, for that matter).

Consider ways you can measure your success after the campaign, and decide those methods before you begin. Otherwise, it can be too easy to manipulate the results. For example, if your goal is to drive traffic, also state that you will track that by measuring the boost in Pinterest referrals to your site during the campaign. Have a concrete percentage increase as a goal. I have more on metrics and tracking statistics in Chapter 11.

Although Pinterest is new, there have been a small number of standout, creative campaigns already. One of my favorites is one that an Israeli agency, Smoyz Creative, did for Kotex.

They sought out a social network where members could express their passions and their inspiration and settled on Pinterest. There, they found 50 women and, based on their pins and boards, came up with what inspires those women. They turned that into a personalized, custom gift for each woman (with a box of Kotex tucked into the gift, of course), and reached out to each member.

To get their present, all the women had to do was repin the pin showing their gift.

Ultimately, a mailing of 50 gifts resulted in buzz not only on Pinterest about Kotex, but was also voluntarily shared on Twitter, Facebook, and Instagram. In the end, they determined the campaign involving just 50 members sparked 2,284 interactions with almost 700,000 impressions. You can find out more about the campaign in a video the agency created on YouTube at `http://youtu.be/UVCoM4ao2Tw`.

Another clever way to market on Pinterest while still being useful for Pinterest users is Sherwin-Williams's Chip It! web application (see Figure 10-2).

Figure 10-2:
The
Sherwin-
Williams
Chip It! site.

Design pins and color palette images are popular on Pinterest. This site, at `http://letschipit.com`, lets you enter the URL for an image. It then generates a paint palette (using Sherwin-Williams paint colors, naturally). You can pin the image for the palette (see Figure 10-3), and when you do, it links to the Chip It! site.

Figure 10-3:
Pinning a
paint palette
from the
Sherwin-
Williams
site.

Both of these examples have something in common. The campaigns don't attempt to mold Pinterest to the brands' marketing goals. Instead, the brands cater to the Pinterest membership and community. They build the buzz naturally, by being interesting and creative. They do not build buzz by shoving it down users' throats, which, on social networks, always backfires.

Deciding Whether to Use Pin It to Win It Campaigns

The first thing marketers do when they see a social network get popular is ask how to take advantage of it, which makes sense. The next thing many do, unfortunately, is create a contest. That is not to say that you can't have a contest, or that they don't have value when done properly.

What I am saying is that this is the lowest level of engagement, and it is the path of least effort. It is also one that can look effective on paper (hey, we got a thousand repins!), but in reality, any gain is short-term and shallow.

There will always be people who will jump through a couple of hoops to win a trinket. Many more will find the whole thing annoying (especially if it is an interruption on a social network). You don't always hear from those people, but believe me when I say that you made an impression.

Before you jump in and launch a Pin It to Win It campaign, consider the pros and cons. If you will do a contest, you should be sure

- ✔ **You don't ask people to jump through too many hoops.** Panera Bread, for example, had a Pin It to Win It contest that required that people follow them, repin their original contest pin, create a board, pin 10 images on a theme while including a special contest hashtag, and finally go to Panera's Facebook page (where you must Like Panera Bread to see content) to submit the board (see Figure 10-4). And the incentive? A chance at winning a $50 Panera gift card. Yes, they got repins, but they also got comments from people who either said it was too much work or were confused by the steps (see the bottom of Figure 10-4).

- ✔ **You have a great prize as incentive.** Again, some people will enter a contest no matter the prize. But for most people, a low dollar-value prize, especially if it requires significant effort, will not perform well.

- ✔ **It is simple to enter.** Don't make people take several steps to enter because many will not bother to begin it. Others get halfway through it, give up, and are annoyed with you for wasting their time.

Figure 10-4: Panera's Pin It to Win It campaign.

✔ **You are not spammy.** In fact, encouraging several repins of one contest image as the Panera contest does may annoy many of a user's friends and followers. Remember that silent group I mentioned earlier who doesn't necessarily complain publicly but is aggravated with your brand nevertheless? If you click the link to Panera's Facebook page (as required by the contest), you get bounced to an intermediary page that indicates several Pinterest users reported the link as spam (see Figure 10-5). There is no way to know how many reports result in this message, but even if you annoy a handful, that might be too many.

✔ **The contest engages and hooks people.** In the Panera example, the themed board idea was a great one (asking "What Makes Your Day Better?"). Look for ways to connect a contest to your company's mission, passions, lifestyle, or something that is more universal and interesting than sharing your products. If you are promoting products, be creative about it. People *do* share products (in fact, Products I Love is one of the main suggested boards when people sign up). Just make it fun and easy for them to share your products (or your posts or whatever you want to promote). When pins are created authentically like that, they don't annoy others and they generate repins.

For example, Gifts.com has a contest that is purely self-promotional. It requires people to pin their favorite products from the Gifts.com site (see Figure 10-6).

Figure 10-5:
A warning that the link to Panera's Facebook page has been reported as spam by Pinterest users.

Figure 10-6:
The Gifts.
com weekly
Pin It to Win
It contest.

I mean, how sales-y is that, right? But this is one of the purely self-promotional contests I like. It is simple to enter. There are no hoops to jump through, no linking a special way, or naming a board after the company. People simply find a product they love on Gifts.com and pin it. Most people can probably find something they genuinely love and would probably pin anyway on a larger site like that.

There isn't even an entry form. Gifts.com is using the source page to find pins each week from their site to pick a winner.

It also is prompting many people to create pins from their site. (I scrolled down their source page a few times to generate new pins from their site, and the pins were still only two days old.) The pins are, presumably, something the pinner really wants, so probably not terribly offensive to that member's followers. This in turn drives traffic to Gifts.com. I am betting it also drives sales — it can be very tempting to buy something when you are browsing around a shopping site.

The bottom line is that you *can* run a contest. I wouldn't view it as the ultimate, highest level of Pinterest marketing available to you, but it can be useful and even wildly successful. A properly planned and executed contest, which takes advantage of the great features of Pinterest without spamming members, can be a quality component of your Pinterest marketing efforts.

Chapter 11

Tracking Pinterest Metrics

In This Chapter

▶ Using site statistics to measure the traffic impact of Pinterest

▶ Using analytics to identify your top influencers

▶ Tracking success over time with a Pinterest report

*W*hatever your reason for marketing on Pinterest, there is likely a way to track whether it's working. Although some people think it is difficult to measure the results of social media efforts, that is actually not true. Pinterest is no exception.

The Pinterest site doesn't offer statistics beyond the very basic (number of followers, for example, or number of repins of a specific pin). There are many other metrics you can check to measure the impact of Pinterest. You can also use analytics to figure out which influencer really drives traffic. It is helpful to track your statistics, especially over time.

For this chapter, I use two popular web analytics programs, Google Analytics (free) and Clicky (free and paid versions). Many statistics and analytics programs are out there, so I can't show them all. Most analytics programs (and certainly all of the decent ones) have at least basic information on referrals and inbound links, so you should be able to use your program to find similar data.

Using Analytics and Statistics Programs to Track Traffic Referrals

If you're using analytic software like Google Analytics (www.google.com/analytics) or Clicky (http://getclicky.com) to monitor your website traffic and other data, you can look at your site's referrals to see total traffic from Pinterest, and you can also dig into those referrals to determine which pins specifically drove a lot of traffic. You can also determine which Pinterest members send you the most traffic by identifying which pins were the top referrers.

You can also compare Pinterest referrals with other popular sites for social sharing, such as Facebook and Twitter. You can examine how visitors from Pinterest behave when they arrive on your site and whether they stick around and visit other pages or they simply drop in and leave quickly.

In this chapter, I show how to find these statistics from two programs that I recommend: Google Analytics (which is free) and Clicky (which is free with limited features below 3,000 daily page views to your site, or operates on a sliding pay scale if you get more traffic and want premium features). Even if you use another statistics program, any decent one includes data on referrals from other sites.

To track Pinterest effectiveness in Google Analytics, follow these steps:

1. **Log in to Google Analytics and select the site you want to examine and then the date range you want to view.**

2. **From the left menu, choose Traffic Sources⇨Sources⇨All Traffic.**

   The All Traffic page appears and shows you how Pinterest compares to all methods of entry to your site, as shown in Figure 11-1. If you have no Pinterest referrals yet, you will not see it in the list.

Figure 11-1:
View all traffic in Google Analytics.

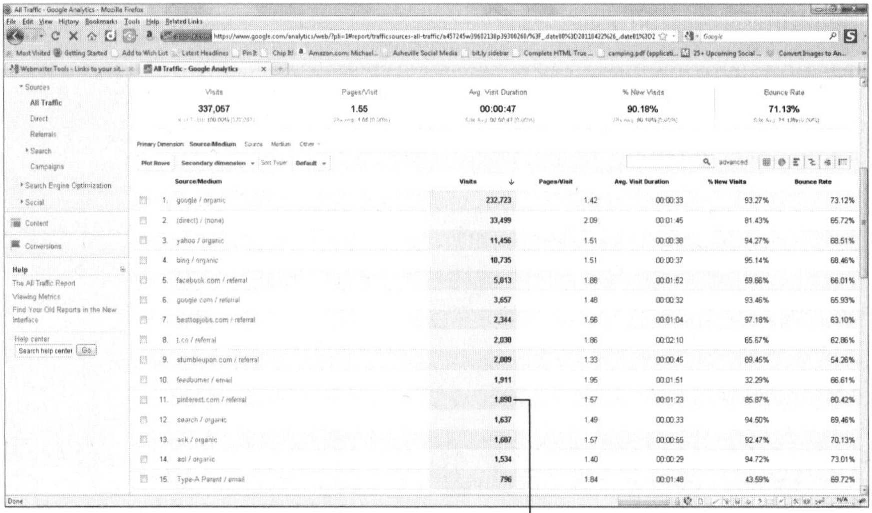

This site has gotten 1,890 hits referred from Pinterest.

3. **Also under Sources, click Referrals.**

   This step eliminates searches and direct site visits and shows you how Pinterest compares to other website referrals. (See Figure 11-2.) You can also view statistics to the right of each referring site on pages per visit, time on site, percentage that were new visitors to your site, and bounce rate. *Bounce rate* is how long someone stays on your site. A lower bounce rate is better than a higher bounce rate because it refers to the percentage of visitors who leave as soon as they arrive.

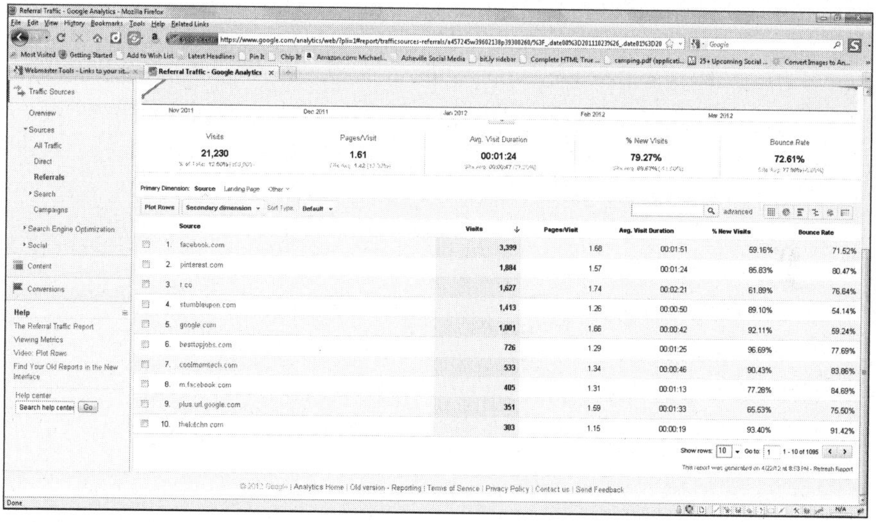

Figure 11-2:
View all referrals in Google Analytics.

4. **From this list, click Pinterest to see a page with a list of deep links on Pinterest that sent traffic to your site as well as total numbers on visitors from each pin. (See Figure 11-3.)**

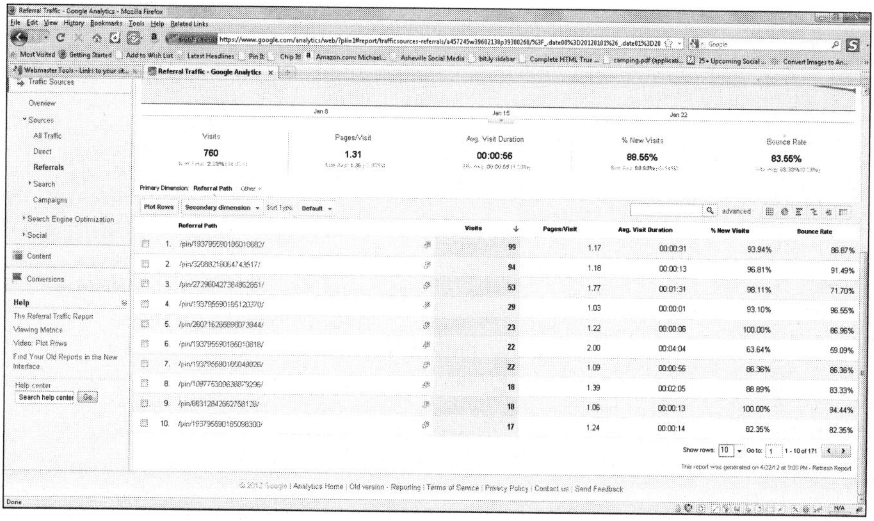

Figure 11-3:
A list of deep links on Pinterest that drove traffic to your site.

 5. Click the arrow to the right of a URL in the list to go to the page on Pinterest and view it.

   You can also click the URL itself in the list to get more details on that page as a referrer.

To track Pinterest referrals in Clicky, follow these steps:

 1. Log in to Clicky and navigate to the site you want to track.

 2. At the top right, set the date range you want to view.

 3. Halfway down the page on the left, look under the Links section.

   You see all incoming links and the traffic totals. (See Figure 11-4.) This list shows you the deep links sending the most traffic.

Figure 11-4:
Incoming
links in
Clicky.

 4. In the Links section, click Domains.

   This shows a list of the domains sending the most traffic. (See Figure 11-5.)

 5. Click pinterest.com.

   This step takes you to detailed statistics about visitors from the site as well as a comparison between Pinterest-referred visitors and all other visitors when it comes to pages per visit, time on site, and bounce rate (see Figure 11-6). If you have a premium account, you can also see the exact pins at the bottom of this screen and the number of referrals for each. Click the arrow to the right of a URL to go to the URL itself, or click the URL to see detailed stats about that inbound referral.

Figure 11-5:
Domain
referrals in
Clicky.

Figure 11-6:
Statistics
on Pinterest
visitors.

Tracking Followers, Repins, and Likes

At the time of this writing, no great tool exists for keeping track of all your repins and likes short of looking at your notifications and your pin pages. I imagine a company (or companies) will soon come up with some robust metrics program.

If you want to do it manually, you need to go to the Pinterest home page while logged in and click your name at the top right. Click Pins to display your latest pins. Below each pin are the individual statistics for that pin (for instance, likes and repins). Obviously, this can be a painful way to track results. It may be better to keep track of your popular pins and watch those for trends in what works and doesn't.

For now, the easiest thing to track is your followers. You can do that by visiting your profile at set time frames (weekly or monthly, for example) and making note of your followers. To do so, visit your profile page by clicking your name at the top right corner. From there, you will see a number followed by Following (see Figure 11-7).

Figure 11-7:
Finding your
number of
followers.

Followers and Following numbers

Creating a Pinterest Measurement Report

Whether you work for a Fortune 500 company and need to answer to a board or you are a sole proprietor running the Pinterest account (and answering only to yourself), it is important to keep an eye on your statistics. It doesn't have to be time-consuming to do so. Tracking metrics helps you identify what works and determine how much time you should dedicate to Pinterest.

If you know your way around Microsoft Excel, you probably already know how to create a basic spreadsheet. For those of you who don't have Excel and/or aren't familiar with Excel, I recommend using Google Documents. It is free and simple to use.

Ideally, a basic report tracks at least the following:

✔ Your followers on Pinterest over time.

✔ Your traffic referrals from Pinterest over time.

Preferably, your report also compares that to the same metrics at other social networks you use. It also compares the clicks per follower ratio.

Here are instructions on how to create a basic report to track Pinterest metrics (as well as other popular social networks). You can feel free to use my sample report (see Figure 11-8), which you can find at `http://bit.ly/pinterestreport`.

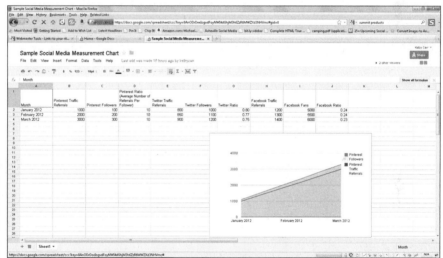

Figure 11-8:
A sample
social media
metrics
report.

When you go to this URL, you must log into Google, click File, and then click Make a Copy. From there, you can save the report into your own Documents account and edit it.

To create this report yourself:

1. **Log into Google and visit the Google Documents site at** `http://docs.google.com`.

2. **At the top left, click the red Create button, and then click Spreadsheet.**

   This takes you to a blank spreadsheet with no title or fields completed.

3. **Click where it says Untitled Spreadsheet, which provides a pop-up window to rename the document (see Figure 11-9).**

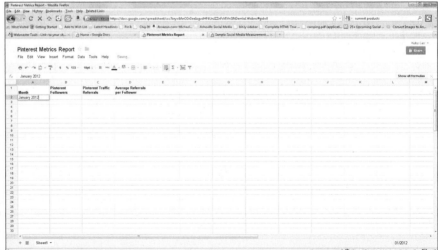

Figure 11-9:
Changing
the docu-
ment's
name.

4. **Enter a new name and click the OK button.**

   You return to the spreadsheet and the new title is at the top.

5. **Double-click in the top left field and type in your date header (for example, Month).**

   You can do this weekly or monthly or in whatever time frame you want to regularly track (see Figure 11-10). I recommend monthly.

   Continue in the next fields to the right entering other headers for the numbers you want to track, such as number of followers and traffic referrals.

Figure 11-10:
Entering
header
fields in your
spread-
sheet.

6. **Move to the next row and enter the data (date and numbers, for example).**

   Keep adding rows for any dates you have data or, if this is your first month of tracking, add your starting data for a single entry.

   If you want to include a column to calculate the ratio of referrals per follower, you can do so by letting the document do the math for you. In Figure 11-11, I do this by entering **=sum(c2/b2)** and pressing Enter. You should replace c2 with the field identifying your total referrals field, and replace b2 with the field identifying your total followers field.

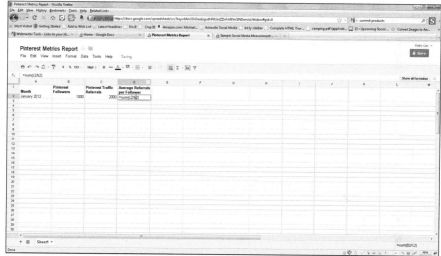

Figure 11-11: Doing a math calculation in your Google spreadsheet.

As you add rows to this spreadsheet, you can double click on the =sum field at the top to generate the same calculation all the way down your spreadsheet. For example, if you later add three more months to your spreadsheet, you can double-click the top month's field and the next three months' math for the ratio of referrals per follower automatically populates.

7. **(Optional) Add a chart to visually display the numbers over time by clicking Insert at the top menu, and then Chart.**

   A Chart Editor dialog box appears (see Figure 11-12). The basic settings pull all of your data into a chart, but you can adjust the settings and chart style as you wish.

8. **Click Insert.**

   You return to your spreadsheet and the chart is there.

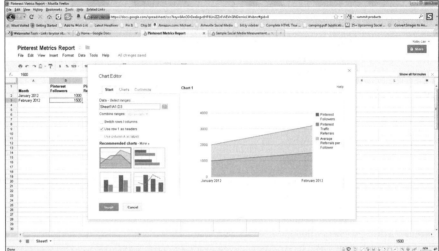

Figure 11-12:
Adding
a chart
to your
spread-
sheet.

9. **Click File at the top left. You can then choose to download the document in a variety of formats (by clicking Download As and then choosing a format), publish it to the web, or e-mail it.**

   Google automatically saves and stores your documents as you edit. You can find your spreadsheet (and other documents) again anytime by visiting http://docs.google.com.

Chapter 12

Ten Pins That Went Viral

In This Chapter

▶ What makes a pin go viral

▶ What it means when a pin goes viral

▶ Tips for going viral

*G*oing viral (and why it happens) can seem like a complete mystery, and sometimes it truly is. On Pinterest, you will find a few common themes. Mouthwatering food is much more likely to go viral, and pins about crafts, beauty, fashion, and home are recurring viral themes.

The implications of going viral can be dramatic if you are lucky enough to be the link connected to a viral pin. It can result in a powerful blast of web traffic, and even translate into a spike in sales.

There is no magic formula for going viral (and odds are good if you try to force it, it won't happen). If you have amazing imagery on your site and you make it easy for people to pin those images, however, you help your chances.

Chocolate Chip Cookie Recipe Pin

One chocolate chip cookie recipe proves a few things about going viral on Pinterest: Your content can be simple, and your content doesn't need to be new (this post is from 2008, and the blog hasn't had a post since 2010).

It doesn't hurt that the alluring chocolate chip cookie image was pinned by a member with almost a million followers, either.

This pin — described as Jacques Torres's Secret Chocolate Chip Cookie Recipe — a *New York Times* best cookie contest winner — got 41,364 repins and 6,329 likes. See Figure 12-1, and find the original pin at `http://pinterest.com/pin/24980972902922359/`.

Figure 12-1:
A chocolate
chip cookie
recipe
pin that
got 41,364
repins.

Harry Potter Light Switch Pin

I am not even sure the founders of Pinterest imagined how many pins would be related to pop culture, but it definitely is a huge segment of Pinterest pinning.

The other interesting thing about this viral pin is that it illustrates the lesson I mentioned earlier in Chapter 9. It is important to watermark your images. The Etsy seller who created this light switch was not pinned as the original source, but Tumblr was because someone shared the image on their Tumblr account. The seller comments to indicate where to find and buy the light switch. If the image had been watermarked, however, anyone who saw the pin would immediately know where to buy it.

The pin — showing a Dumbledore quote on a light switch, which I *love* — had 10,005 repins and 2,167 likes. See the pin in Figure 12-2, and find the original at http://pinterest.com/pin/3307399695979064/.

Bed and Breakfast Bathroom Pin

One bathroom looked amazing enough for at least 36,772 people to repin it. The bathroom, which is in the 1900 Inn on Montford in my hometown of Asheville, NC, is featured on BedandBreakfast.com and went viral at least twice on Pinterest.

Figure 12-2:
A Harry
Potter light
switch that
got more
than 10,000
repins.

The first viral pin of the inn's image got 19,385 repins and 2,833 likes (see Figure 12-3). You can find the pin at `http://pinterest.com/pin/200128777160877935/`. The second pin of the same image got 17,387 repins and 2,359 likes. You can find it at `http://pinterest.com/pin/11540542764999107/`.

Figure 12-3:
This image
of an
upscale
bathroom at
an inn went
viral twice
for a total
of 36,772
repins.

Pretty Updo Pin

This simple pin shows that sometimes all it takes is pretty to go viral. The person who originally pinned this is a woman in Croatia with 951 followers, not exactly a power influencer on Pinterest.

Yet the image she pinned has been repinned 43,754 times and liked 2,402 times.

I think this is great news for those of you who are new to Pinterest. Unlike some social networks where your influence is heavily based on how many friends or followers you have, I frequently see pins go viral that were shared by a regular, average Pinterest member.

You can see the pin in Figure 12-4 at http://pinterest.com/pin/69383650478661626/.

Figure 12-4:
A pretty updo image that was repinned 43,754 times.

He's Quite Perfect Pin

There are a few things the popularity of this pin illustrates. One, it shows how well-received images with quotes are on Pinterest. Many members (myself included) have entire boards dedicated to quotes. You will probably find that anytime you pin something with an especially moving or funny quote, it is more likely to get repinned than other image types.

My theory is this: People love to pin quotes on Pinterest for the same reason you love to pin quotes on a real pinboard or over your desk. They remind you what's important or they give you a chuckle on a long, hard day.

Lastly, this quote proves that quality (and correctness) doesn't always matter. This quote has a typo right in the middle (I cringe!), yet the meaning was powerful enough that 42,398 people repinned it. Surely, some of them caught the typo and repinned it anyway. That also makes the case that you really needn't take yourself (or your brand) too seriously on Pinterest. It is a place to have fun.

You can see the pin in Figure 12-5, or find it on Pinterest at http://pinterest.com/pin/3166662207836841/.

Figure 12-5:
Even a
typo wasn't
enough
to keep
this image
from being
repinned
42,398 times.

Balsamic Watermelon Cubes Pin

Food pins are a common theme among viral pins (as you will notice in this chapter and on the site). The pin is popular because it is food, yes, but also because it is at once simple and elegant. It is being pinned by everyone from foodie moms who want to try it at home to couples who want to show it to their wedding caterers.

What I like about the pin is that it didn't simply go viral once, but was pinned repeatedly. By that, I mean that there are several instances of someone pinning the image and getting anywhere from a handful to a few hundred repins (see Figure 12-6).

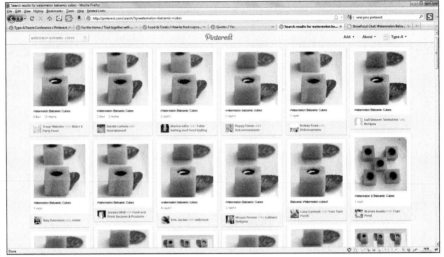

Figure 12-6:
The
Watermelon
Balsamic
Cubes
has been
pinned and
repinned
repeatedly.

I didn't find a single instance with tens of thousands of repins, but instead found dozens of pins that each had repins. In Figure 12-7, for example, the pin had 1,255 repins and 286 likes. You can also find the pin at http://pinterest.com/pin/46584177365531388/.

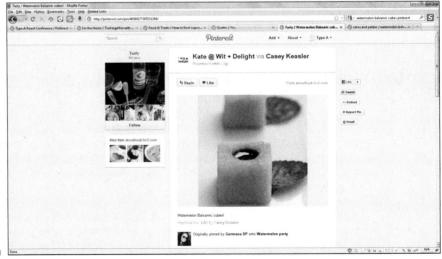

Figure 12-7:
One of
the many
Watermelon
Balsamic
Cubes pins
received
1,255 repins.

How to Frost a Cupcake Pin

It's clear that food pins thrive on Pinterest, but this viral pin demonstrates another type of content as well that performs remarkably on Pinterest. Yes, it is food-related, but this cupcake pin also connects to a detailed video tutorial. Great pins not only show a wonderful and informative image, but they also connect people via a click to even better information. That is the case with this pin.

The pin, shown in Figure 12-8, got 13,569 repins and 657 likes. You can also see it at `http://pinterest.com/pin/198862139765594935/`.

Figure 12-8:
The How to Frost a Cupcake pin was repinned 13,569 times.

How to Make a Clementine Candle Pin

Again, this pins shows that tutorials are popular. This pin also shows again the importance of branding or watermarking your images. The original pinner made a common etiquette faux pas (one that is also a copyright concern). They directly uploaded the image from Apartment Therapy's site instead of pinning it from the site so it connected to the instructions and the full content.

If you visit the pin online at Pinterest, you will see that several people are frustrated because they try to follow the image-only instructions (which are obviously meant to be a teaser, and a visit to the source site is required for detailed instructions). There are also a few people repeating more detailed instructions or linking to the original content. The pinner also described the basis for this craft as an orange, but commenters explained it must be a Clementine to work.

The good news for Apartment Therapy is that they have their site name prominently displayed on the image. Even with tens of thousands of repins, people can find the source of the image (and the instructions) pretty easily.

The pin received 45,360 repins and 2,018 likes. You can see the pin in Figure 12-9, or see it on Pinterest at http://pinterest.com/pin/282530576592856960/.

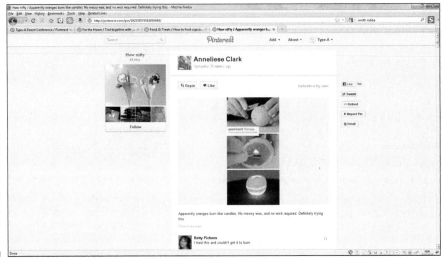

Figure 12-9:
The How
to Make a
Clementine
Candle
pin was
repinned
45,360 times.

Water Candle Pin

The fascinating thing about this viral pin is that sometimes all it takes is for an image to look good. This wasn't pinned by an influencer (she has 69 followers). It doesn't connect to a detailed tutorial, or even to a place to buy the lovely water candle décor. It simply shows an idea for something pretty for your house. That's it.

It was enough to prompt 18,969 people to repin it, and to generate 2,952 likes. You can see the pin in Figure 12-10 or at http://pinterest.com/pin/30047522483618866/.

Figure 12-10:
A water
candle
pin was
repinned
18,969 times.

Camibands Pin

On many social networks, sharing products is considered spammy or inappropriate. The cool thing about Pinterest, especially for marketers, is that people are organically sharing their favorite products constantly. When they do, it oftentimes doesn't feel like a commercial. Instead, it feels like your friend saying, "Psst! Check out this cool thing I found today."

The other great thing is that you don't have to be a household name to stand out on Pinterest. Etsy (www.etsy.com), for example, is one of the most pinned domains and its site features independent sellers, usually with handmade items.

The Camibands story is another example of a small business success story on Pinterest. Holly Xerri, creator of Camibands, said her business started as a hobby. It's a small business based exclusively online. One day, she was unexpectedly overwhelmed with orders. She assumed her product must have appeared in a major magazine or TV show. It turns out that pins of it went viral.

When her product was worn on the *Today* show, for example, her site saw a spike of 3,500 page views. When it went viral on Pinterest, she got more than 40,000 page views in four days from Pinterest alone.

There were several pins of the Camiband (some with just a few repins, and some with thousands). You can see a pin in Figure 12-11 that had 4,212 repins and 1,213 likes, or you can find it on Pinterest at `http://pinterest.com/pin/134756213819955483/`.

Figure 12-11:
The Camiband pins went viral, driving more than 40,000 page views to the online shop in four days.

Index

• *Symbols* •

#keyword in pin description, 36. *See also* hashtags
@ symbol in pin description, 36, 124
[pinit] short code, 141

• *A* •

account profile, Pinterest
  accessing, 71, 168
  bio, 32–33
  editing, 31–34
  e-mail preferences, 33
  Facebook account, connecting to, 26, 53, 54–55
  information in, 27
  picture, 31–32
  places to share, 58, 122
  setting up, 28–31
  tracking followers via, 168
  Twitter account, connecting to, 26
accounts, e-mail, 25
accounts, Facebook
  advantages of connection with Pinterest, 26
  app authorization, 51–52, 56
  completing Pinterest registration via, 26–27
  connecting to, 26, 50
  finding Pinterest members, 24, 25
  Follow All option, 52–53
  following friends, 50–55
  integrating with Pinterest, 53, 55
  inviting friends to join Pinterest, 50
  liking boards, 116
  limitations on connecting, 50
  logging in via, 54
  on multiple profiles, 53, 54–55
  pinning images from, inability to, 144
  pins, liking, 116–117

pins, sharing, 84, 88–89
Pinterest compared, 1, 6
promoting Pinterest page, 115
refreshing profile picture from, 32
social sharing plug-in, 138–140
timeline, integrating Pinterest into, 89, 115
accounts, Pinterest
  for bloggers, 19
  business, 19, 55
  controlling, 25–26
  for crafters, 19
  creating, 17, 26–28
  hacking, 26
  hiring someone to run, 21–22, 25
  multiple, 17, 18, 20–21
  password, changing, 54
  personal, 18, 19, 20
  preventing problems, 25–26
  responsibility for, 20–22, 25
  security, 26
  for sole proprietors, 19
activities, Pinterest, 34, 95, 96–97
Add dialog box, 64
alerts, e-mail, 33–34
Alexa demographic data, 8, 9
Artwork, Pinterest, 117–118
@ symbol in pin description, 36, 124
avatars, 31–32

• *B* •

bad behavior, online, 34, 130, 132, 155
Balsamic Watermelon Cubes pin, 177–178
beautiful pins, 129
beauty pins, 173
Bed and Breakfast bathroom pin, 174–175
behavior, Pinterest. *See also* tracking Pinterest metrics
  etiquette, 34–35, 132
  inappropriate, 34, 130, 132

Betty Crocker, board topics, 60
billboards, promoting Pinterest page on, 117
bio, profile, 32–33
Bitly link shortener, 120–121
bloggers, Pinterest accounts for, 19, 20
blogs
  checking for Pinterest links, 57, 58
  linking to, 32
  promoting Pinterest page on, 106–107, 115
  social sharing plug-ins, 138
  statistics on pins, 134
Board Category field, 63
boards
  about, 5, 35, 59
  Betty Crocker, 60
  business, on personal account, 18, 19, 20
  business card topic, 11
  categories, browsing, 63, 87
  category selection, 63
  changing to group, 69–70
  cover photo, 72–74
  creating, 63–64, 81, 96
  creating initial, 29, 30
  deleting, 76
  deleting suggested, 29
  description, 29, 64
  editing, 75
  editing name/description, 29
  example, 6
  filling with pins, 79
  following, 37
  General Electric Badass Machines board, 12
  general-topic, 60
  group, 64, 65–66, 69–70, 76–77
  information sharing, 12
  Lance Crackers, 60, 61
  liking on Facebook, 116
  Lilly Pulitzer retail store board, 14
  Lindt Chocolate, 60, 61
  Little Debbie Dessert Sushi, 12, 13
  maintenance, 96
  naming, 29, 61, 62, 63
  pins, minimum number, 60
  Pinterest For Dummies, 4
  Pinterest Marketing For Dummies, 4
  places to share, 58, 122
  rearranging, 71–72
  renaming, 62, 75
  Scholastic, 13, 59
  searching, 41
  selecting for pins, 81
  for self-promotion, 62
  sharing on social networks, 116
  Sony Electronics, 12, 13, 62
  specific-topic, 60
  suggested, 29
  Today show's peacock, 60
  topics, 59–62
  transferring to different account,
    inability, 20
  unfollowing, 28, 37
  URLs, 62, 116
  The Weather Channel Personalities, 11, 12
bounce rate, 165
brand awareness, increasing, 9
brand enthusiasts, 10, 153–154
Brand New Sony Products board, Sony
    Electronics, 62
branding images, 146–147
broadcast marketing, promoting Pinterest
    page on, 117–118
broadcasting level of engagement,
    124–125, 126
browsing
  Everything, 45–46, 88
  Gifts, 88, 93
  Popular pins, 44, 45, 88, 127
Build-a-Bear Workshop accounts, 20–21
business accounts, Pinterest, 19, 55
business cards
  board topic, 11
  promoting Pinterest page on, 117, 119
businesses
  benefits of Pinterest to, 6–7
  goal setting, 9–10
  identity, described, 17–18
  on Pinterest, examples, 10
  promotion, boosting, 10
  sharing personality of, 6, 10–14
  use of personal Pinterest accounts,
    18, 19, 20
  website, driving traffic to, 6, 9

• C •

Cabot Cheese Pinterest account, 125, 126
Camibands pin, 181–182
campaigns, Pinterest marketing. *See also* tracking Pinterest metrics
  approach to, 153, 155, 158
  goals, 156
  measuring results, 156
  Pin It to Win It, 1, 124, 156, 158–161
  purpose, 119
  successful, examples, 157–158
  turn-offs, 155–156
Carr, Kelby, 1–4, 10
categories, board, 63, 87
CEOs, responsibility for account, 21–22
Chip It! web application, Sherwin-Williams's, 157–158
chocolate chip cookie recipe pin, 173–174
Clark, Maxine, 20, 21
clickable, making words, 36, 90–91
clicks, tracking, 112, 113, 115, 120
Clicky analytics program, 112, 163, 164, 166–167
clothing pins, 99, 173
Cold Brew Labs Pinterest app, 95–96, 97
collaborative boards
  about, 64
  adding collaborators, 69–70
  benefits, 70
  creating, 69–70
  ineffective, 65
  inviting collaborators, 65
  removing collaborators, 77
  removing yourself from, 76–77
  signup form, sample, 65–66
  uses, 69
collage tool for cover photos, 74
collages, 146
color palette images, 158
comments
  about, 100
  benefits, 100, 128
  for engagement, 124
  following conversations on pins, 102

  getting to, 128–129
  from home page, 101
  linking to content in, 100
  negative, 132, 133, 155
  offensive, 130, 132
  from pin pages, 101–102
  pins that encourage, 128–129
  politeness, 100–101
  process, 100–101
  from search results, 101
  self-promotion in, 100
  time needed, 96
Compete demographic data, 8
complaints, handling, 132, 133, 155
confirmation e-mail, 22–23
Connect page, 118
content
  already on Pinterest, finding, 133–135
  encouraging better, 7
  finding unexpected, 7
  Google search for, 154
  importance of good, 133
  making easy to pin, 135–137
  permalinks for, 136
  quality, characteristics of, 97
  types successful as pins, 98–100
contests, Pin It to Win It, 1, 124, 156, 158–161
controversial pins, 129
conversations in comments
  about, 100
  benefits, 100, 128
  for engagement, 124
  following conversations on pins, 102
  getting to, 128–129
  from home page, 101
  linking to content in, 100
  negative, 132–133, 155
  offensive, 130, 132
  from pin pages, 101–102
  pins that encourage, 128–129
  politeness, 100–101
  process, 100–101
  from search results, 101
  self-promotion in, 100
  time needed, 96
cool product pins, 99

copyright
  fair use standard, 15
  Pinterest issues, 14, 34, 84
  Pinterest policies, 15
  reporting violations, 130, 149–151
  resources on, 15
Copyright Complaint Form, 150–151
copyright symbol, typing, 149
cost, displaying on pins, 88, 92–93
cover photo, board, 72–74
craft pins, 98, 173
crafters, accounts for, 19
Crafty Mama of 4 linkups, 122
creating
  accounts, Pinterest, 17, 26–28
  boards, 29–30, 63–64, 81, 96
  content, 126–127
  group boards, 69–70
  pins, 79–81, 83–84, 144
  repins, 86–87
  spreadsheets, 68
creativity, rewards of, 12, 59, 153, 158
crediting images, 34
custom Pinterest icons, 107
cute pins, 129

● D ●

debates, heated, 130, 132
décor pins, 99, 158, 173
demographics of Pinterest users, 8–9, 22
descriptions
  board, 29, 64
  image, 14
  pin, 36, 124
design pins, 99, 158, 173
Digg, Pinterest compared, 5
Digg Digg social sharing plug-in, 138
DIY pins, 98, 127
Doctor Who pins, 99
domain, finding pins from, 88, 143, 154

● E ●

e-blasts, promoting Pinterest page on,
  112–115
Edit Board Cover button, 73

Edit Board screen, 75
e-mail
  account for Pinterest, 25
  alerts, 33–34
  confirmation messages, 22–23
  finding friends to follow, 55–57
  Follow All option, 57
  inviting collaborators, 69
  notifications, 37, 102
  preferences, setting, 33–34, 102
  promoting Pinterest page, 112–115
emotional responses to pins, 127
employees, responsibility for account, 22, 25
engagement
  barriers to, 123
  benefits, 123
  with customers, increasing, 6, 10–14
  example of pin, 125
  importance, 123
  levels, 124–126
  methods, 124
  in Pinterest, 95
engager level of engagement, 125–126
enthusiasts, brand, 10, 153–154
essential tasks, 96
etiquette, Pinterest, 34–35, 132
Etsy site, 181
evangelists, brand, 10, 153–154
event pins, 99
Everything stream, 45–46, 88
Excel spreadsheets, creating from forms, 68
Experian's Hitwise blog, 8

● F ●

Facebook
  advantages of connection with Pinterest, 26
  app authorization, 51–52, 56
  completing Pinterest registration via,
    26–27
  connecting to, 26, 50
  finding Pinterest members, 24, 25
  Follow All option, 52–53
  following friends, 50–55
  integrating with Pinterest, 53, 55
  inviting friends to join Pinterest, 50
  liking boards, 116

limitations on connecting, 50
logging in via, 54
on multiple profiles, 53–55
pinning images from, inability to, 144
pins, liking, 116–117
pins, sharing, 84, 88–89
Pinterest compared, 1, 6
promoting Pinterest page, 115
refreshing profile picture from, 32
social sharing plug-in, 138–140
timeline, integrating Pinterest into, 89, 115
fashion pins, 99, 173
Fashionable Chocolate board, Lindt
     Chocolate, 60, 61
File Upload dialog box, 85
finding unexpected content, 7
5minutesformom linkup, 122
flyers, promoting Pinterest page on, 119
Follow All option, 37, 39–41, 52–53, 57
Follow Me on Pinterest buttons, 57–58,
     106–107
followed boards, 37
followed members. *See also* friends to
     follow, finding prospective
  about, 36
  automatic selection, 28
  boards, 37
  browsing stream, 87
  for engagement, 124
  etiquette, 34
  number, limitations on, 40
  process, 39–42
  selecting members, 29, 38–39
  unfollowing, 28, 49
  via Facebook, 50–55
  viewing, 47, 49–50
followers
  about, 36
  adding, 37, 96
  buying, 38
  e-mail notifications of new, 37
  finding friends via, 47–48
  finding potential, 105
  following back, 37, 48, 49–50
  gaining, 38
  limitations on connecting to, 53–54

making name linkable, 36, 124
  preparing for, 105
  proportion of number following, 40, 48, 58
  tracking, 168
  viewing, 47
Followers page, 48
follower-to-following ratio, 40, 48, 58
following conversations on pins, 102
food pins, 98, 173, 177
form, Copyright Complaint, 150–151
forms, 65–68
Formsite.com, for collecting collaborators, 65
freelancers, responsibility for account, 20
friends to follow, finding prospective
  e-mail contacts, 55–57
  Facebook, 50–55
  finding Everything stream, 45–46
  on Pinterest, 24
  searching for, 38–43
  using categories, 42–44
  via existing friends, 47–48
  via followers, 48–50
  via Popular pins, 42, 44–45
  via social networks, 57
fun, importance of, 12

• *G* •

Game Day board, Betty Crocker, 60
General Electric Badass Machines board, 12
general-topic boards, 60
Get Pinspired linkup, 122
Gifts, 88, 93
Gifts.com contest, 160–161
glitches in Pinterest, 34
Gmail, searching for friends to follow,
     55–57
Goodies page, 82
Google Adplanner, 8
Google Alerts, 7
Google Analytics, 9, 163–166
Google Documents, 65–68, 168–172
Google Forms, 66–68
Google image search, pinning images from, 34
Google search for Pinterest content, 154.
     See also no-follow coding

group boards
  about, 64
  adding collaborators, 69–70
  benefits, 70
  creating, 69–70
  ineffective, 65
  inviting collaborators, 65
  removing collaborators, 77
  removing yourself from, 76–77
  signup form, sample, 65–66
  uses, 69

• *H* •

hacksplice tool for cover photos, 74
hairstyle pin, 176
handmade goods, sellers of, 19
Harry Potter light switch pin, 174–175
Harry Potter pins, 99
hashtags, 36, 90–91
He's Quite Perfect pin, 176–177
Hitwise blog, 8
home page
  about, 37
  commenting from, 101
  latest activity, viewing, 34
  pinning to, 79
How to Frost a Cupcake pin, 179
How to Make a Clementine Candle pin,
    179–180
how-tos, pins connected to, 127, 179
HTML coding in bio, 32
humor pins, 99

• *I* •

icons, book, 3–4
icons, Pinterest
  custom, 107
  follow me, 57–58, 106–107
  print-friendly, 117
identity, choosing type, 17–19
images
  board cover, 72–74
  branding, 146–147

collages, 146
color palette, 158
company logos, 144
copyright violations, 130, 149–151
crediting, 34
cropping, 73
descriptions, 14
editors, 147–149
from Facebook, inability to pin, 144
finding URL for, 137
formats, 144
full-size, 15
interesting, characteristics of, 126–128
liking, 36
links to image, including, 85–86
making easy to pin, 137
misuse of, handling, 146–150
optimizing for Pinterest, 143, 145–146
pinnability, checking for, 144
pinned, locations appearing, 35
pinning, 6, 34, 35, 96, 124
pinning, blocking, 7, 14, 144, 149, 151–152
Pinterest logos, 57–58, 106–107, 117
of products, sharing, 13
quotes as, 98
reviewing, importance, 73
sample promotional, 84
text, adding to, 145
troubleshooting, 144
uploading, 32, 84–85
watermarking, 145–149
from websites, 81
in real life (IRL), promoting Pinterest page,
    118–121
infographic pins, 99, 127
information sharing boards, 12
interests, specifying in profile, 28–29
interns, responsibility for account, 22
invitations
  checking spam folder for, 23
  for group collaborators, 69
  issuing to friends, 24
  mass, avoiding, 50, 56
  methods for getting, 22
  from Pinterest members, 24
  requesting, 22–23

starting account creation from, 27
via Facebook, 50
iPhone app, 95, 97
IRL (in real life), promoting Pinterest page,
  118–121

• *J* •

Jacques Torres's Secret Chocolate Chip
  Cookie Recipe, 173–174
Javascript code for making web content
  pinnable, 135–137
joke pins, 99
.jpg image format, 144

• *K* •

Kotex marketing campaign, 157
Kraft's e-mail newsletter, 112

• *L* •

Lance Crackers boards, 60, 61
landing page for Pinterest promotion,
  118, 119
legal issues, Pinterest, 14–15
Lemons with a Pea artwork, 154
Like button, on pin page, 103
likes, Facebook, 116–117
likes, Pinterest
  about, 36, 102
  for engagement, 124
  image, 36
  as interaction, 102
  process, 103
  repins compared, 102
  time needed, 96
  tracking, 102, 168
Likes filter, turning on, 102
Lilly Pulitzer retail store board, 14
Lindt Chocolate, Fashionable Chocolate
  board, 60–61
Lindt Chocolate identity, 17–18
link shortener tools, 120–121
linkups, 58, 122

linky posts, 58, 122
Little Debbie Dessert Sushi board, 12–13
logging in, 18, 54, 80
logos, image format of company, 144
logos, Pinterest
  custom, 107
  follow me, 57–58, 106–107
  print-friendly, 117

• *M* •

MailChimp e-mail marketing company,
  113–115
marketing on Pinterest. *See also* tracking
  Pinterest metrics
  approach to, 153, 155, 158
  goals, 156
  measuring results, 156
  Pin It to Win It, 1, 124, 156, 158–161
  purpose, 119
  successful, examples, 157–158
  turn-offs, 155–156
Martha Stewart Pinterest account,
  124–125, 126
Mashable, as friend source, 58
measurement report, Pinterest, 168, 169
member view, of self-promotion, 34
members, Pinterest. *See also* followed
  members; followers
  determining which generate most
    traffic, 163
  finding specific, 88
  invitations from, 24
  removing from group boards, 77
  searching for, 42
  tagging in pins, 91–92
  unfollowing, 28
mentions, 36, 124
metrics, tracking Pinterest
  account promotions, 112–113, 115, 120
  effectiveness, 164–166
  followers, 168
  importance, 168
  information available, 163–164
  likes, 102, 168
  measurement report, 168–169

metrics, tracking Pinterest *(continued)*
  news, 7
  on Pinterest site, 163
  repins, 167–168
  tools for, 112, 163–167
  website referrals, 164–166
mobile phones, 95–97, 119

• N •

names, selecting board, 61, 62
negative feedback, 132–133, 155
news boards, 12
news coverage on Pinterest, 7
newsletters, promoting Pinterest page on
    e-mail, 112–115
Nielsen Wire, 8
no-follow coding, 7, 14
notifications
  of form submission, 68
  of new followers, 37
  setting up, 102

• O •

outfit pins, 99, 173
outsourcing, Pinterest management,
    21–22, 25
owner of business, responsibility for
    account, 21–22

• P •

Panera Bread contest, 159–160
password, changing, 54
peacock board, *Today* show, 60
peak Pinterest activity, timing, 96
people on Pinterest. *See also* followed
    members; followers
  determining which generates most
      traffic, 163
  finding specific, 88
  invitations from, 24
  removing from group boards, 77

searching for, 42
  tagging in pins, 91–92
  unfollowing, 28
permalinks, 79, 136
personal identity, 17–18
personal Pinterest accounts, 18–20
personality, sharing business, 6, 10–14
photos, board cover, 72–74
Photoshop Elements image editor, 147–149
picmarkr watermark tool, 145
picture, profile, 31–32
Pin Etiquette recommendations, 35. *See
    also* etiquette, Pinterest
Pin It button
  about, 36, 82
  adding pins with, 83–84, 96
  adding via WordPress, 136–138
  example display, 83
  installing, 82–83
  plug-ins, 138, 141–143
  for website, 30, 36, 135–137
Pin It button plug-in, standalone, 138,
    141–143
Pin It Friday linkup, 122
Pin It to Win It marketing campaigns, 1,
    124, 156, 158–161
Pin Me! linkup, 122
pin pages
  commenting from, 101–102
  features available on, 101
  getting to, 101
  optimizing images for, 145
pinboards
  about, 5, 35, 59
  Betty Crocker, 60
  business, on personal account, 18–20
  business card topic, 11
  categories, browsing, 63, 87
  category selection, 63
  changing to group, 69–70
  cover photo, 72–74
  creating, 63–64, 81, 96
  creating initial, 29, 30
  deleting, 76
  deleting suggested, 29

description, 29, 64
editing, 75
editing name/description, 29
example, 6
filling with pins, 79
following, 37
General Electric Badass Machines board, 12
general-topic, 60
group, 64–66, 69–70, 76–77
information sharing, 12
Lance Crackers, 60, 61
liking on Facebook, 116
Lilly Pulitzer retail store board, 14
Lindt Chocolate, 60–61
Little Debbie Dessert Sushi, 12, 13
maintenance, 96
naming, 29, 61–63
pins, minimum number, 60
Pinterest For Dummies, 4
Pinterest Marketing For Dummies, 4
places to share, 58, 122
rearranging, 71–72
renaming, 62, 75
Scholastic, 13, 59
searching, 41
selecting for pins, 81
for self-promotion, 62
sharing on social networks, 116
Sony Electronics, 12–13, 62
specific-topic, 60
suggested, 29
Today show's peacock, 60
topics, 59–62
transferring to different account, inability, 20
unfollowing, 28, 37
URLs, 62, 116
The Weather Channel Personalities, 11–12
[pinit] short code, 141
pinning images
about, 35
for engagement, 124
etiquette, 34
Google image search, 34
process, 6
time needed, 96

pins. *See also* repins
about, 5, 35
commenting, characteristics that encourage, 128–129
controversial, 129
creating from websites, 79–81, 83–84
creating manually, 144
creating to home page, 79
on deleted boards, 76
descriptions of, 36, 124
on domain, finding, 133–135
enhancing, 90–93
finding company-related, 154
finding interesting, 87–88
following conversations on, 102
interesting, characteristics of, 126–128
minimum number per board, 60
pages, 101–102, 145
places to share, 58, 122
popularity, 44
price tags on, 88, 92–93
quality, characteristics of, 98
reporting offensive, 130–131
searching, 38–40
selecting board for, 81
self-promotional, recommended maximum number, 79
sharing on social media, 88–89, 116–117
sources, finding, 135
tagging member names, 91–92
types of content, 98–100
uploading images as, 84–85
video, 83, 87
viewing statistics on, 127, 128
Pinterest
about, 5
benefits for business, 6–7
Facebook/Twitter compared, 1, 6
history, 1
popularity, 1, 6–7
Pinterest app, 95–97
Pinterest Block, 152
Pinterest For Dummies board, 4
Pinterest For Dummies (Carr), pins on, 155
Pinterest Marketing For Dummies board, 4
Pinterest Marketing For Dummies (Carr), 1–4

Pinterest mobile, 95–96
Pinterest Profile Linkup for parents, 122
Pinterest recommendations on self-
    promotion, 35
Pinterest search
  boards, 41
  commenting from results of, 101
  for company-related pins, 154
  members, 42, 88
  pins, 38–40
  using hashtags, 90
Pinterest sharing plug-ins, 137–141
Plemmons, Robin, 154
plug-ins
  about, 144
  for adding Pinterest link, 106, 108–112
  pin blocking, 144, 152
  Pin It button, 138, 141–143
  Pinterest sharing, 137–140
  RSS Widget, 108–112
  social sharing, 137–140
  Twitter, 138–140
  watermark, 145
  WordPress, 137–139
.png image format, 144
politeness, importance, 100–101
Polyvore fashion site, 99
pop culture pins, 99
Popular page, 44–45, 88, 127
Popular pins, repinning, 45
postcards, promoting Pinterest page on, 119
posts
  links directly to, 79, 136
  linky, 58, 122
  on Pinterest, 7
  places to share, 122
  posting non-self-promotional, 34
  sharing, 58, 122
  tutorials, 127, 146, 179
#keyword in pin description, 36
power users, 155
prettified tool for cover photos, 74
Pretty Updo pin, 176
price tags on pins, 88, 92–93
print marketing, promoting Pinterest page
    on, 117–119

prizes, contest, 159
product pins, successful types, 99
products, sharing images of traditional, 13
professionals, responsibility for account, 20
profile, Pinterest
  accessing, 71, 168
  bio, 32–33
  editing, 31–34
  e-mail preferences, 33
  Facebook account, connecting to, 26,
    53–55
  information in, 27
  picture, 31–32
  places to share, 58, 122
  setting up, 28–31
  tracking followers via, 168
  Twitter account, connecting to, 26
profile linkups, 58, 122
promoting page. *See also* campaigns,
    Pinterest marketing
  on billboards, 117
  on blog, 106–107, 115
  in broadcast marketing, 117–118
  on business cards, 117, 119
  clicks, tracking, 112–113, 115, 120
  costs, 106
  in e-mail, 112–115
  landing page, 118–119
  in linkups, 122
  preparing for, 105
  in print marketing, 117–119
  with QR codes, 119
  in real life, 118–121
  on receipts, 119
  on signage, 119
  on smartphones, 119
  on social networks, 115–117
  on website, 106–107
promotion, self-
  boards for, 62
  in comments, 100
  images, 84
  limiting, 79
  member view of, 34
  Pinterest recommendations on, 35
promotion of business, boosting, 10

promotions, marketing. *See also* tracking
    Pinterest metrics
  approach to, 153, 155, 158
  goals, 156
  measuring results, 156
  Pin It to Win It, 1, 124, 156, 158–161
  purpose, 119
  successful, examples, 157–158
  turn-offs, 155–156
puzzle-style tool for cover photos, 74

• Q •

QR codes, promoting Pinterest page
    with, 119
QR Stuff code generator, 119–120
Quantcast demographic data, 8
quirky product pins, 99
quote pins, 98, 176–177

• R •

radio, promoting Pinterest page on, 117
Really Simple Social Facebook Twitter
    Share Buttons social sharing plug-in,
    138–140
rearranging boards, 71–72
receipts, promoting Pinterest page on, 119
recipe pins, 98, 173, 177
referrals, website, 163, 164–166
registration screen, Pinterest, 27
Remember icon, 3
reminders to use Pinterest, 97
repins
  about, 5, 36, 86, 102
  buying, 38
  creating, 86–87
  for engagement, 124
  finding pins for, 87–88
  getting list of, 134
  likes compared, 102
  motivations for, 86
  Popular pins, 45
  time needed, 96
  tracking, 167–168
  viewing statistics on, 127, 128

reporting bad behavior, 132
results, tracking Pinterest
  account promotions, 112–113, 115, 120
  effectiveness, 164–166
  followers, 168
  importance, 168
  information available, 163–164
  likes, 102, 168
  measurement report, 168–169
  news, 7
  on Pinterest site, 163
  repins, 167–168
  tools for, 112, 163–167
  website referrals, 164–166
RSS Widget plug-in, 108–112
rude behavior, 34, 130, 132, 155

• S •

scheduling Pinterest activity, 96–97
Scholastic boards, 13, 59
search, Pinterest
  boards, 41
  commenting from results, 101
  commenting from results of, 101
  for company-related pins, 154
  members, 42, 88
  pins, 38–40
  using hashtags, 90
search engine optimization (SEO), 7, 14
search engines, use for Pinterest content,
    7, 14, 154
searching for friends to follow, 38–43, 55–57
searching Twitter for keyword *Pinterest,* 57
self-promotion
  boards for, 62
  in comments, 100
  images, 84
  limiting, 79
  member view of, 34
  Pinterest recommendations on, 35
SEO (search engine optimization), 7, 14
serendipity, Pinterest for fostering, 7
Share As Image tool, 98
Shareaholic, 6
Sharing is Caring social sharing plug-in, 138

sharing pins as engagement, 124
sharing responsibility for Pinterest, 97
She Promotes linkup page, 122
Sherwin-Williams's Chip It! marketing
    campaign, 157–158
short codes, 141, 143
signage, promoting Pinterest page on, 119
signup form, sample group, 65–66
smartphones, 95–97, 119
Smoyz Creative marketing campaign, 157
social media. *See also* Facebook; Twitter
  choosing for sharing plug-ins, 139
  pins about, 127
  Pinterest ranking in popularity, 1
  prioritizing, 133
  promoting page on, 115–117
  sharing buttons recommended for, 138
social media company, using to manage
    Pinterest, 21–22, 25
social media manager, responsibility for
    account, 22
Social page, 118
social sharing plug-ins, 137–138
Social Sharing Toolkit social sharing
    plug-in, 138
soldier with baby pin, 127–128
sole proprietors on Pinterest, 19–20
Sony Electronics boards, 12–13, 62
Sony on Sale board, Sony Electronics, 62
spam, 34, 132
specific-topic boards, 60
SpinPicks app, 95
spreadsheets
  creating from forms, 68
  in Google Documents, 169–172
Star Wars pins, 99
stores, promoting Pinterest page in, 118–121
StumbleUpon, Pinterest compared, 5
SurveyMonkey.com, for collecting
    collaborators, 65
symbols, book, 3–4

• T •

tagging member names in pins, 91–92
talker level of engagement, 125

Technical Stuff icon, 4
terminology, Pinterest, 35–36
Terms of Service, Pinterest, 14–15
text
  adding to images, 145
  pinning, 98, 176–177
themes, form, 68
time for Pinterest, 95–96
timeline, integrating Pinterest into
    Facebook, 89, 115
times of peak Pinterest activity, 96
Tip icon, 3
Today show's peacock board, 60
trackable links, 120–121
tracking Pinterest metrics
  account promotions, 112–113, 115, 120
  effectiveness, 164–166
  followers, 168
  importance, 168
  information available, 163–164
  likes, 102, 168
  measurement report, 168–169
  news, 7
  on Pinterest site, 163
  repins, 167–168
  tools for, 112, 163–167
  website referrals, 164–166
traffic to business site, driving, 6, 9
trolls, 130, 132, 155
troubleshooting images not pinnable, 144
Tumblr, pinning images from, 34
tutorials
  collage images for, 146
  pins connected to, 127, 179
TWC (The Weather Channel) Personalities
    board, 11, 12
Twitter
  advantages of connection with Pinterest, 26
  completing Pinterest registration via,
    26–27
  connecting to profile, 26
  hashtags, differences from Pinterest, 90
  limitations on connecting to, 50
  plug-ins, 138–140
  promoting Pinterest page on, 115
  refreshing profile picture from, 32

searching for keyword *Pinterest,* 57
settings for sharing plug-ins, 139
sharing pins on, 88–89, 116–117
tweeting a pin, 84
typeaparent page, 10, 58, 122

• U •

unfollowing boards, 37
unfollowing members, 28
updates, accessing, 34
URLs
 in bio, 32
 for boards, 62, 116
 changes to, 62, 75
 finding pins from, 88
 for images, 137
 linking to, 32, 120
 pinning with, 79–81, 83–84
 for pins, 116
 Pinterest, finding, 116
 shortener tools, 120–121
user profile, Pinterest
 accessing, 71, 168
 bio, 32–33
 editing, 31–34
 e-mail preferences, 33
 Facebook account, connecting to, 26,
  53–55
 information in, 27
 picture, 31–32
 places to share, 58, 122
 setting up, 28–31
 tracking followers via, 168
 Twitter account, connecting to, 26
username, Pinterest, 27, 88
users, Pinterest. *See also* followed
  members; followers
 determining which generates most
  traffic, 163
 finding specific, 88
 invitations from, 24
 removing from group boards, 77
 searching for, 42
 tagging in pins, 91–92
 unfollowing, 28

• V •

videos, 83, 87
violations of copyright, 130, 149–151
viral pins
 about, 173
 Balsamic Watermelon Cubes pin, 177–178
 Bed and Breakfast bathroom pin, 174–175
 Camibands pin, 181–182
 chocolate chip cookie recipe pin, 173–174
 Harry Potter light switch pin, 174–175
 He's Quite Perfect pin, 176–177
 How to Frost a Cupcake pin, 179
 How to Make a Clementine Candle pin,
  179–180
 Pretty Updo pin, 176
visual sharing of business story, 6

• W •

Warning icon, 3
Water Candle pin, 180–181
Watermark RELOADED plug-in, 145
watermarks, 145, 146–149, 174, 179–180
watermarktool.com watermark tool, 145
The Weather Channel (TWC) Personalities
  board, 11, 12
websites. *See also* URLs
 author, 10
 checking for Pinterest links, 57
 driving traffic to, 6, 9
 embedding forms on, 68
 finding from pins, 135
 finding pins from, 88, 143, 154
 making content easy to pin, 135–137
 Pin It button, 36, 135–137
 pinning images from, 81
 pinning pages, 79–81, 83–84
 promoting Pinterest page on, 106–107
 referrals to, 163–166
 statistics on pins to, 134
 visitors from Pinterest, tracking
  behavior, 164
wedding pins, 99
Whoopie Pie board, Betty Crocker, 60

widget, adding Pinterest, 108–112
WordPress
  adding Pin It button, 136–138
  adding Pinterest using, 106, 108–112
  blocking pinning on, 152
  dashboard, accessing, 141
  plug-ins, 137–139
  watermark tools for, 145
Wurm, Michael, 155

Xerri, Holli, 181

Yahoo! Mail, searching for friends to
  follow, 55–57

Zoomsphere, as friend source, 58

ple & Mac

ad 2 For Dummies,
d Edition
8-1-118-17679-5

hone 4S For Dummies,
Edition
8-1-118-03671-6

d touch For Dummies,
d Edition
8-1-118-12960-9

c OS X Lion
r Dummies
8-1-118-02205-4

ogging & Social Media

yVille For Dummies
8-1-118-08337-6

cebook For Dummies,
Edition
8-1-118-09562-1

m Blogging
r Dummies
8-1-118-03843-7

itter For Dummies,
d Edition
8-0-470-76879-2

rdPress For Dummies,
Edition
8-1-118-07342-1

usiness

sh Flow For Dummies
8-1-118-01850-7

vesting For Dummies,
Edition
8-0-470-90545-6

Job Searching with Social Media For Dummies
978-0-470-93072-4

QuickBooks 2012
For Dummies
978-1-118-09120-3

Resumes For Dummies,
6th Edition
978-0-470-87361-8

Starting an Etsy Business
For Dummies
978-0-470-93067-0

Cooking & Entertaining

Cooking Basics
For Dummies, 4th Edition
978-0-470-91388-8

Wine For Dummies,
4th Edition
978-0-470-04579-4

Diet & Nutrition

Kettlebells For Dummies
978-0-470-59929-7

Nutrition For Dummies,
5th Edition
978-0-470-93231-5

Restaurant Calorie Counter
For Dummies,
2nd Edition
978-0-470-64405-8

Digital Photography

Digital SLR Cameras &
Photography For Dummies,
4th Edition
978-1-118-14489-3

Digital SLR Settings & Shortcuts
For Dummies
978-0-470-91763-3

Photoshop Elements 10
For Dummies
978-1-118-10742-3

Gardening

Gardening Basics
For Dummies
978-0-470-03749-2

Vegetable Gardening
For Dummies,
2nd Edition
978-0-470-49870-5

Green/Sustainable

Raising Chickens
For Dummies
978-0-470-46544-8

Green Cleaning
For Dummies
978-0-470-39106-8

Health

Diabetes For Dummies,
3rd Edition
978-0-470-27086-8

Food Allergies
For Dummies
978-0-470-09584-3

Living Gluten-Free
For Dummies,
2nd Edition
978-0-470-58589-4

Hobbies

Beekeeping
For Dummies,
2nd Edition
978-0-470-43065-1

Chess For Dummies,
3rd Edition
978-1-118-01695-4

Drawing For Dummies,
2nd Edition
978-0-470-61842-4

eBay For Dummies,
7th Edition
978-1-118-09806-6

Knitting For Dummies,
2nd Edition
978-0-470-28747-7

Language & Foreign Language

English Grammar
For Dummies,
2nd Edition
978-0-470-54664-2

French For Dummies,
2nd Edition
978-1-118-00464-7

German For Dummies,
2nd Edition
978-0-470-90101-4

Spanish Essentials
For Dummies
978-0-470-63751-7

Spanish For Dummies,
2nd Edition
978-0-470-87855-2

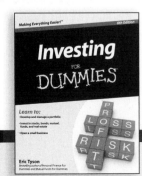

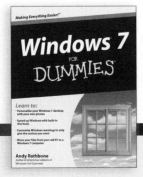

Math & Science

Algebra I For Dummies,
2nd Edition
978-0-470-55964-2

Biology For Dummies,
2nd Edition
978-0-470-59875-7

Chemistry For Dummies,
2nd Edition
978-1-1180-0730-3

Geometry For Dummies,
2nd Edition
978-0-470-08946-0

Pre-Algebra Essentials
For Dummies
978-0-470-61838-7

Microsoft Office

Excel 2010 For Dummies
978-0-470-48953-6

Office 2010 All-in-One
For Dummies
978-0-470-49748-7

Office 2011 for Mac
For Dummies
978-0-470-87869-9

Word 2010
For Dummies
978-0-470-48772-3

Music

Guitar For Dummies,
2nd Edition
978-0-7645-9904-0

Clarinet For Dummies
978-0-470-58477-4

iPod & iTunes
For Dummies,
9th Edition
978-1-118-13060-5

Pets

Cats For Dummies,
2nd Edition
978-0-7645-5275-5

Dogs All-in One
For Dummies
978-0470-52978-2

Saltwater Aquariums
For Dummies
978-0-470-06805-2

Religion & Inspiration

The Bible For Dummies
978-0-7645-5296-0

Catholicism For Dummies,
2nd Edition
978-1-118-07778-8

Spirituality For Dummies,
2nd Edition
978-0-470-19142-2

Self-Help & Relationships

Happiness For Dummies
978-0-470-28171-0

Overcoming Anxiety
For Dummies,
2nd Edition
978-0-470-57441-6

Seniors

Crosswords For Seniors
For Dummies
978-0-470-49157-7

iPad 2 For Seniors
For Dummies, 3rd Edition
978-1-118-17678-8

Laptops & Tablets
For Seniors For Dummies,
2nd Edition
978-1-118-09596-6

Smartphones & Tablets

BlackBerry For Dummies,
5th Edition
978-1-118-10035-6

Droid X2 For Dummies
978-1-118-14864-8

HTC ThunderBolt
For Dummies
978-1-118-07601-9

MOTOROLA XOOM
For Dummies
978-1-118-08835-7

Sports

Basketball For Dummies,
3rd Edition
978-1-118-07374-2

Football For Dummies,
2nd Edition
978-1-118-01261-1

Golf For Dummies,
4th Edition
978-0-470-88279-5

Test Prep

ACT For Dummies,
5th Edition
978-1-118-01259-8

ASVAB For Dummies,
3rd Edition
978-0-470-63760-9

The GRE Test For
Dummies, 7th Edition
978-0-470-00919-2

Police Officer Exam
For Dummies
978-0-470-88724-0

Series 7 Exam
For Dummies
978-0-470-09932-2

Web Development

HTML, CSS, & XHTML
For Dummies, 7th Edition
978-0-470-91659-9

Drupal For Dummies,
2nd Edition
978-1-118-08348-2

Windows 7

Windows 7
For Dummies
978-0-470-49743-2

Windows 7
For Dummies,
Book + DVD Bundle
978-0-470-52398-8

Windows 7 All-in-One
For Dummies
978-0-470-48763-1

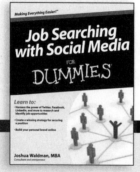

Wherever you are in life, Dummies makes it easier.

From fashion to Facebook®, wine to Windows®, and everything in between, Dummies makes it easier.

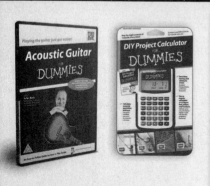